Praise for *How to Live*

"This is a timely book for troubled times, showing how the values and practices established by St. Benedict in the 6th century can help us lead happier lives. A self-professed workaholic, the author allows the reader to see how her life has changed for the better since she took this ancient wisdom to heart."

Kathleen Norris, author of *The Cloister Walk, Dakota: A Spiritual Geography, Acedia and Me*, and *Saving Grace*.

"To have such a gifted writer live and report through the lens of *The Rule of St. Benedict* is a blessing for all of us. Judith Valente offers more than perspective. Her life's work is monastic. To read, reflect and report is the role of a professional journalist. As an author and journalist, Valente has *The Rule of Benedict* for her editor. What a gift for us."

Mary Margaret Funk, author of *Thoughts Matter; Tools Matter; Humility Matters;* and *Out of the Depths.*

"Judith Valente has a knack for making the ancient Rule of Benedict come alive as a guidebook for today. With many examples and personal anecdotes, her presentation is insightful, delightful, and very honest. You will find yourself chuckling, but then checking to see where you've been hit."

Jerome Kodell, author of *Don't Trust the Abbot: Musings from the Monastery* and *Life Lessons from the Monastery.*

"Like all of Judith Valente's writing, this beautiful actualization of the Rule of St. Benedict is accessible, inviting, challenging, inspiring and wise. Even if you've never once set foot in a Benedictine monastery, this boo... ...ered life in the bu... ...grimage.

For Thomasita Homan, OSB,
who brought me to The Rule.

And, as always,
for my husband, Charley.

HOW
TO
LIVE

What the Rule of St. Benedict Teaches Us
About Happiness, Meaning, and Community

JUDITH VALENTE

Foreword by
JOAN CHITTISTER, OSB

Afterword by
MARTIN E. MARTY

WILLIAM
COLLINS

William Collins
An imprint of HarperCollins*Publishers*
1 London Bridge Street
London SE1 9GF

WilliamCollinsBooks.com

First published in Great Britain in 2018 by William Collins
This William Collins paperback edition published in 2019

This edition published by arrangement with Hampton Roads Publishing Company,
Inc. Charlottesville, VA 22906. Distributed by Red Wheel/Weiser, LLC

1

A catalogue record for this book is available from the British Library

ISBN 978-0-00-830830-8

Cover design by Heike Schuessler
Interior by Maureen Forys, Happenstance Type-O-Rama

Typeset in Adobe Garamond Pro and Trajan Pro

Printed and bound by CPI Group (UK) Ltd, Croydon CR0 4YY

MIX
Paper from
responsible sources
FSC
www.fsc.org FSC™ C007454

This book is produced from independently certified FSC™ paper
to ensure responsible forest management.

For more information visit: www.harpercollins.co.uk/green

CONTENTS

ACKNOWLEDGMENTS

I wish to express gratitude to Lisa Breger and Annie Parker for being early readers of the manuscript; Mary Lou Kownacki, OSB, Mary Ellen Plumb, OSB, and Anne McCarthy, OSB for reviewing the manuscript for accuracy; Joan Chittister, OSB for her insightful introduction; Kathleen Norris, Macrina Wiederkehr, OSB, and Mary Margaret Funk, OSB for their inspirational work on *The Rule*; Jane Hagaman of Red Wheel/Weiser and Addie Talbott for their careful editing; Greg Brandenburgh of Hampton Roads Publishing, without whose vision the book would not be possible; my agent, Amanda Annis of Trident Literary Agency, for her unwavering belief in this project; Ray Clem of Atchison for his cheerful support of me and all things Benedictine; the Benedictine sisters of Mount St. Scholastica for modeling *The Rule* for me; and my beautiful husband, Charles Reynard, for being my best editor and best friend.

Editor's Note: The epigraphs in this book are all taken from *The Rule of St. Benedict*. The chapter titles are noted in each one.

Translations of *The Rule* are adapted from *A Reader's Version of The Rule of St. Benedict in Inclusive Language*. Edited by Marilyn Schauble, OSB and Barbara Wojciak, OSB. Benetvision. 1989.

FOREWORD

The United States, young and bustling, new to the world, and racing to become something fresh and meaningful, is impatient with age. We are a living experiment in innovation and uniqueness. Europe and other older civilizations, on the other hand, are studies in transformation and tradition. They don't bulldoze the past to put up something new; they build on it from within and in the process make way for the new even as they preserve the old. Clearly, the underlying difference between the character of American cities and the cast and quality of European cities is obvious: it is the way each of these cultures deals with time.

The distinction is worth contemplating on more levels than one. The lesson to be considered here has as much to do with spiritual awareness as it does with architecture. It has something to tell us about the way we all view time.

Time is a continuum of empty ages filled only by the substance we bring to it ourselves. The temptation of every age is to discount the old, to worship at the shrine of the new. But the value of time lies as much in what we ourselves bring to the understanding of time as it does in what time brings to us. It is our awareness and interpretations of time that determine our own place in the development of the human spirit, of the spiritual impact of yesterday on tomorrow.

The deep down spiritual truth is that time is always and forever an invitation to growth. Whether the wisdom of the ages shapes us, or not, determines the nature of our civilization, the depth of our culture, the spiritual filter through which we ourselves, in our own time, mold the character of the world around us. If, as individuals, we understand time as the storehouse of our souls, explore it for answers to perennial questions, and test it for its value, then we stand to become the bearers of the wisdom of the ages. If not, we simply join the ranks of societies before us that walked through life untouched by time. We become one more excursion through epochs we failed to fathom, and so end devoid of the substance they were meant to bring us.

And yet, if we make the effort to trace the chain of life and thought and ideals that have brought us as a people from one moment in history to another, we make ourselves part of the passage to a healthy tomorrow. We are prepared, then, to go in our own times—where there is no road—and leave a path.

This book helps us see what we are losing; to make us taste what we're in danger of dismissing as unimportant. It reminds us of what we've missed but is still at hand, waiting to enliven the age in which we live as well as to be remembered for its contribution to the past.

This book, written in a period of political turmoil and personal angst, of national division and individual uncertainty, recalls us to the best of ourselves. It details for us the basis of good society. It brings us beyond the roiling headlines of the day to a consciousness of the little things that make for human community, healthy families, moral maturity, and personal peace and happiness.

But to do that, it takes us back to the thinking of the 6th century. It translates a moment of social upheaval for us and identifies a point of spiritual eruption, the impact of which still marks the world. Most importantly of all, it asks whether or not the ideas that lifted eras before us out of darkness might be exactly what we need now to restore our own best selves in the here and now.

The document this book expounds as a guide for modern living is Benedict of Nusia's *Rule* for monastics. Written in the 6th century, it is still one of the preeminent spiritual treatises, a veritable guarantee of the good life. But why?

Because of its glorious, even extreme, asceticism? No, though it certainly models self-control.

Because of its rigorous prayer life? No, despite its commitment to regular and profound immersion in the mind of God.

Because of its demanding solitude and silence? Hardly, given all its concern for the upbuilding of the human community.

Then why? In a word: simplicity. Because of its attention to our undying desire to be truly happy. It describes for us what it takes to create genuine human community. It challenges us to find balance in the face of destructive competition. It encourages us to sharpen our commitment to cultivate the meaningful in life. It enables us to renew in ourselves the appreciation of humility in a world of narcissistic excess.

Or, to put it another way, it deals now, as then, with the likelihood of daily life to fray our nerves and wear down our early commitment to make everything in life a spiritual experience. Indeed, who among us does not need a spiritual path to lead us through the undergrowth of modern life, to heighten our consciousness of the sacred in the secular, to become whole?

Roman society knew the cost of war, the foolishness of debauchery, the stifling engorgement of excess on every level. Benedict's simple rule of life became a template for living, authentic to the core and a guide to the highest of spiritual heights through the ages. Yet always simple. Always genuine. Always truly human.

This book takes us to the heart of life—our own as well as the ideas of others. Judith Valente gives us the opportunity to plot our own lives and struggles against that of an ancient spirituality that has been the basis of life for thousands in the last fifteen centuries and is a torch for many still.

It is a book worth reading. Better yet, it is a book worth thinking about.

—JOAN CHITTISTER, OSB, AUTHOR OF *THE RULE OF BENEDICT*

1

YEARNING FOR LIFE

On Beginning

Is there anyone here who yearns for life and desires to see good days?
—FROM THE PROLOGUE TO *THE RULE OF ST. BENEDICT*

This is a book about living. Not about surviving, but living a balanced, meaningful, and attentive life. It is like a traveler's trunk that contains all the wisdom I wish I had acquired earlier in my life and seek now to pass on.

I can't take credit for originating these ideas. They come from the mind of a teacher who lived more than fifteen hundred years ago. He originally wrote his guide, or *Rule*, for people living in a monastic community. Monasteries might seem like an unlikely source of wisdom for those of us living in the age of Instagram. And yet, this slender text has proved indispensable to people throughout the centuries seeking to live a saner, more

How to Live

peaceful life *outside* of a monastery. For me—a working journalist, an often overburdened professional, and a modern married woman—it has been a constant companion, never far from my work desk or nightstand.

The Rule of St. Benedict emerged from an era when a great civilization was under threat from violent outside forces. The economy favored the wealthy. Social norms were changing, and political leaders lacked the public's trust. Many blamed their anxiety on government, foreigners, or those of a different religion or race. Sound like the nightly news? Welcome to Rome in the 6th century.

St. Benedict was not a priest or a religious official. He was, however, a leader—a young man disillusioned with the conflict, greed, injustice, and lack of compassion he saw around him. He believed the gospels offered a wiser, more consequential way to live. He called himself and his followers "monks," from the Greek *monos*, meaning one. It signaled they had one goal, to seek God and forge a new kind of society with single-minded devotion. The society Benedict and his monks constructed rested firmly on counter-cultural pillars.

Buffeted by war, Benedict didn't amass an army. He sought to build community. Instead of the false security of personal wealth, he endorsed the freedom of simplicity. His solution to daily threats of violence was to counsel his monks to sleep without their knives. To cope with the chaos around him, he embraced silence. He said: Replace grumbling with a sense of gratitude. Start each day with praise. Seek the common good and your own well-being will follow.

Community. Simplicity. Humility. Hospitality. Gratitude. Praise. These are the pillars of Benedictine spirituality. These are the things that matter. This is perhaps what we've forgotten.

2

Often it feels as though a genie of discord has escaped into the very air we breathe, liberating us to be our worst selves. We just have to read the news. A group of young men convene near the US White House, chanting "*Heil* victory, *Heil* our people," and raise the fisted Nazi salute. African-American middle school students are greeted with shouts of "Go back to Africa." Strangers pull off the head scarves of Muslim women out shopping. Gay men hear taunts of "faggot" in the street. White supremacists bearing guns, clubs, and torches march in the center of American cities.

The Rule of St. Benedict invites an alternative vision. It is summed up in a single line from one of the shortest chapters in *The Rule:* "The Good Zeal of Monastics." *Try to be the first to show respect to the other, supporting with the greatest patience one another's weaknesses of body or behavior.* This is the *good* St. Benedict says we are called to model. He asks us to nurture it zealously, *with fervent love*.

One of the most critically acclaimed fantasy films in recent years was a piece of science fiction called *The Arrival*. It is the story of beings from outer space who arrive on earth, igniting a wildfire of fear across the planet. Their language is unlike anything spoken or written, and it includes a unique perception of time. An expert linguist is tapped to initiate contact. If she cannot draw out the visitors' true intentions, the nations of the world will pool their weaponry and launch an all-out assault.

To show her own peaceful motives, the linguist enters the spacecraft, and at considerable risk to herself, removes her biohazard suit. She approaches the strange, multi-limbed creatures with palms open and outstretched. Her body language demonstrates she isn't there to attack. Slowly, by immersing herself in the aliens' language, she uncovers their purpose. Earth escapes an interplanetary disaster, not by superior weaponry or even acts of daring, but by bravely communicating with those we don't at first understand. Success through empathy. In many ways, the film mirrors the parallel society the Benedictine *Rule* calls us to forge. One where the ability to listen, to communicate, and ultimately to understand delivers us from self-destruction.

> *"Who will dwell in your tent, O God? Who will find*
> *rest in your holy mountain? (Ps 15:1) . . ." "Those who*
> *walk without blemish and are just in all dealings;*
> *who speak truth from the heart and have not practiced*
> *deceit; who have not wronged another in any way, nor*
> *listened to slander against a neighbor." (Ps 15:2–3)*
>
> —FROM THE PROLOGUE

The Benedictine *Rule* is as much a text for the spiritual beginner as it is for the spiritually mature. Some have described it as a guidepost. I like to think of it as a railing I can grab onto to steady myself when I encounter a dark, uncertain path. My own journey toward *The Rule* was hardly a direct route. A friend who is a Presbyterian minister recommended the text to me at a time when I had just moved back to the US from Europe and was embarking on a new phase of my writing career. He thought it might satisfy some of the spiritual unrest I was experiencing over whether I was doing enough with my life.

I thought it contained some lovely and thought-provoking passages. *Listen with the ear of the heart . . . Day by day, remind yourself you are going to die. Hour by hour, keep careful watch over all you do . . . Your way of acting must be different from the world's way.* There was also enough in the text that was strange and puzzling to prompt me to set it aside for nearly a decade. It wasn't until I saw *The Rule* lived in the daily context of a contemporary Benedictine monastery that I realized: here was the path I had been seeking.

Atchison, Kansas, is a city I had never thought about, much less visited, before I received an invitation to give a talk on *Touching the Sacred through Poetry* at the retreat center of Mount St. Scholastica, one of Atchison's two Benedictine monasteries. The offer came at a pivotal time for me, both professionally and personally. I had been married only two years. While my marriage was a blessing, I struggled as a second wife to forge a relationship with my two adult stepdaughters.

My first book, *Twenty Poems to Nourish the Soul*, had just come out, and that was another gift. But it, too, came with stresses. I began receiving requests from across the country to lead poetry workshops and retreats on weekends, all the while working my day job at the time as a contributing correspondent for PBS-TV and Chicago Public Radio. I arrived at Mount St. Scholastica on a Saturday night exhausted—physically, mentally, and emotionally. In fact, I felt like a fraud. I wondered how I was going to stand in front of a retreat group the next morning and talk about nourishing the soul when I hadn't fed my own soul a decent meal in weeks.

The morning I was to give my talk, I sat alone in the monastery's oak-lined chapel. Sunlight streamed in through the chapel's distinctive blue stained glass windows. Silence saturated the room. I looked up at the window in front of me. There was St. Benedict with outstretched arms. Surrounding him were some words in Latin: *omni tempore silentio debent studere*. I reached back to the Latin I had studied in college and did a rough translation: at all times, cultivate silence.

Suddenly, the paradox I had been living was staring me the face. I had been running around the country talking and talking, trying to help other people live a more contemplative life, when my own life was missing moments of silence and solitude in which I could simply listen and be.

The Mount sisters seemed keepers of a kind of secret. They balanced work with leisure, laughter with silence, work with prayer. I discovered that everything they do—from the way they eat to how they wash dishes, speak to one another, care for their sick, pray in chapel, and go about their daily work—comes from St. Benedict's *Rule*. Though I didn't know it then, the line that had mesmerized me that morning in the chapel—*omni tempore silentio debent studere*—comes from *The Rule*. What these sisters had, I wanted. I arrived at Mount St. Scholastica a poetry expert of sorts. I left a student of *The Rule*.

"There are days that define your story beyond your life," the female linguist in *The Arrival* says at the beginning of the film. I felt that all of my past somehow had led me to this monastery on a hill and that the Benedictine *Rule* was reaching out to me from the ages.

Over the course of the next three years, I returned repeatedly to Mount St. Scholatica, mining *The Rule* for ways I could apply monastic values and practices to my daily life as a wife, stepmother, writer, and journalist. Benedict asks a pointed question in the book's prologue: *Is there anyone here who yearns for life and desires to see good days?* I wanted to shout, "Yes. Me. Here. Now!"

> *What, dear brothers and sisters, is more delightful than this voice of the Holy One calling to us. See how God's love shows us the way to life.*
>
> —FROM THE PROLOGUE

To delve deeply into *The Rule* is to discover just how astutely Benedict was writing in the 6th century. Recent discoveries about how the brain works buttress ideas he espoused before neuroscience was even a word. Paul Zak is an economist and brain researcher who has studied the effect on the human psyche of a powerful hormone called oxytocin. This is the chemical released in lovemaking, in women who have just given birth, as well as in people who have just acted in some way that benefits others. Zak calls oxytocin "the morale molecule."

Using a variety of research experiments, Zak found that those who give usually end up receiving in return. One person's generosity can even increase the oxytocin levels in another. In other words, human beings appear hardwired for community. We prosper most when we extend trust and receive it in return. The economic models we learn in MBA programs would have us believe the opposite—that self-interest is the fundamental human motivator. Zak, by contrast, found that trusting and exhibiting generous behavior leads to reciprocal generosity and trust.

"The most important factor in determining whether or not a society does well or is impoverished," Zak concluded, "is not natural resources, education, quality health care, or even the work ethic of its people. What matters most in determining outcomes is actually trustworthiness—a moral consideration."

This sounds a good deal like the community Benedict sought to create, and the one he entrusts us to build today. He foresaw the dangers of radical self-interest of the kind that led to the economic meltdown of 2008 and to the Great Depression (as well as other economic crises before and since then), to practices like slavery and apartheid, and to so many of the world's wars. *No one is to pursue what he judges better for himself* to the detriment of others.

This Benedict counseled nearly two millennia before oxytocin was even discovered.

The Rule also has a message for those of us on call twenty-four seven, swirling in a maelstrom of email, texting, Twitter, and Snapchat. It beckons as a plea for balance. Benedict carved the monastic day into distinct periods for work, prayer, reading, leisure, and rest. He believed there is a time to work, and a time to stop work. As someone who has long suffered from a dual diagnosis of workaholic and overachieverism, *The Rule* showed me that it is possible to pause, to care for myself, and still be productive. With its focus on balance, *The Rule* helps orient my attention toward the sacred in the ordinary. It propels me to *live* every day.

In many ways, Benedict and his predecessors—the early monastics of the Egyptian desert—were among history's first psychologists. They understood that in order to live in community—or even as hermits—they would have to confront the emotional demons that haunt us all. They discovered ways to leaven our natural tendencies toward anger, self-absorption, greed, depression, unhealthy appetites, and obsessions. They did this not by repressing those tendencies, but by recognizing we are not our thoughts and we are not our feelings. We can redirect our thoughts and feelings into constructive actions. Doing this allows us to confront life's inevitable turbulence with equanimity. The emotional tools that *The Rule* lays out have been more valuable to me than any self-help book or therapy session.

The reflections in the pages that follow are my attempts to draw out the major themes of *The Rule* in practical takeaways that can lead to personal transformation. For many centuries, men and women who entered monasteries were expected to memorize *The*

Rule in the same way they committed to memory the Psalms or traditional prayers. But as the Benedictine writer Mary Margaret Funk points out, *The Rule* is not something to be absorbed intellectually. It has to be lived. It has to take up residence in our inner life.

"Benedict's great insight," she writes in her memoir *Out of the Depths,* "was that the work of the monastery was not simply about men and women living apart from society in a community. The true work lay in how one developed the interior life."

The happy news is that this also applies to people who don't live in monasteries—people like you and me who are trying to nurture a family, succeed in a rapidly changing workplace, and grow old with a sense of purpose. The true monastic enclosure is the human heart.

> *While there is still time, while we are in this body and have time to accomplish all these things, let us run and do now what will profit us forever.*
>
> —FROM THE PROLOGUE

Happily too, St. Benedict promises to demand of us *nothing harsh, nothing burdensome.* He reminds us we are always only beginners on the path to a deeper interior life. The spiritual journey is not a flight on a supersonic jet, but a slow steady trek, like hiking the Appalachian Trail or walking El Camino de Santiago de Compostela. "The spiritual life is this," a monastic elder from the Egyptian desert once said, "I rise and I fall. I rise and I fall."

I used to think of monastic life as a hopeless throwback to the past, a case of let the last monk or sister standing turn out the lights. Now I look upon it as a window to the future we desperately need in our society: one that stresses community over competition, consensus over conflict, simplicity over self-gain, and silence over the constant chatter and distractions of our lives. And so we begin.

Is there anyone here who yearns for life and desires to see good days?

2

LISTEN WITH THE EAR OF THE HEART

On Paying Attention

Listen carefully my daughter, my son to my instructions and attend to them with the ear of your heart. This is advice from one who loves you; welcome it and faithfully put it into practice.

—FROM THE PROLOGUE

A few years ago, I had the opportunity to report on a talk that Supreme Court Justice Sonia Sotomayor gave to University of Illinois law students. It was not long after the sudden death of her colleague on the court, Justice Antonin Scalia. Scalia often sparred with Sotomayor and the other judges of the court's so-called "progressive" wing. In one of his more colorful opinions, he accused opposing justices of engaging in the "jiggery-pokery" of devious behavior. He derided another majority opinion, of which Sotomayor was a part, as the equivalent of legal "applesauce."

For her part, Sotomayor described Scalia as "the brother I loved, and sometimes wanted to kill." How then, asked one of the law students, did the justices engage in these intense disagreements and still manage to collaborate? Sotomayor gave a very Benedictine answer. They listen to one another.

"You may not like what they're proposing, but that doesn't mean they're doing it from an evil motive," she said of her fellow jurists. Justices can passionately disagree, she said, "and still see the goodness in one another." She offered a recommendation for dealing with professional—and personal—divisions. Less talking, more listening.

I've often marveled, that the first word of *The Rule of St. Benedict* isn't pray, worship, or even love. It's *listen*. This small, unobtrusive word speaks in a whisper. To anyone who studies Benedictine spirituality, the phrase *listen . . . with the ear of the heart* becomes so familiar we can easily lose sight of how revolutionary it is. Listening in the Benedictine sense is not a passive mission. Benedict tells us we must *attend* to listening. In some translations of *The Rule*, we are to actively *incline* ourselves toward it, and nurture it in our everyday activities. Listening is an act of will.

When I look at the failures and disappointments in my own life, I can often trace them to an operator error in listening—usually my own. Even though I earn my living as a journalist—which is to say I listen to other people's stories for a living—in my private life I'm often like the doctor who is her own worst patient. I'm great at hearing my heart's desire, but not so adept at hearing the messages I need to receive from others.

Perhaps it comes from being the youngest in my family and having had to fight to be heard. I am also a person of strong opinions. That too can be a prescription for tone-deafness. Once, a colleague whom I respect called me on a Saturday morning to tell me he thought I can come across too forcefully at staff meetings. My initial reaction: ridiculous! My second reaction was anger that someone I considered a friend would engage in what I felt was a personal attack.

Then I started listening with the ear of my heart. I mentally replayed the tapes of some recent meetings where I had voiced my opinion. I heard my own voice. I could see that what I might consider passionately advocating for a position, others might find argumentative and condescending.

A friend who is a counselor once suggested that when my husband and I disagree on something, instead of repeatedly hammering at our individual opinions, we might stop and each repeat to the other what he or she has said, ending with the question, "Am I understanding you correctly?" It's amazing how many times I have to repeat what my husband has said before I get it right, and he must do the same. We listen through the echo chamber of our own perceptions. The Benedictine *Rule* calls us to not only listen, but to actually hear.

> *Obedience is a blessing to be shown by all, not only to the prioress or abbot, but also to one another, since we know that it is by way of this obedience that we go to God.*
>
> —FROM CHAPTER 71, "MUTUAL OBEDIENCE"

Listening cracks open the door to another Benedictine concept from which most of us would rather run,—that of obedience. My first reaction is to recoil from the word. It conjures memories of being sent to my room or the principal's office for not doing what I was told. Obedience comes from the Latin, *oboedire,* to give ear, to harken, to listen. The Benedictine writer Esther de Waal says that obedience moves us from our "contemporary obsession with the self," and inclines us toward others. For those living in a monastery, obedience isn't merely a rigor to endure. St. Benedict describes it as gift—*a blessing to be shown by all.* In doing so, he moves beyond the common understanding of the word as solely an authoritarian, top-down dynamic. He stresses instead *mutual obedience,* a horizontal relationship where careful listening and consideration is due to each member of the community from each member, as brothers and sisters. *It is by this way of obedience,* he says, *that we go to God.*

In our western civilization, this is a counter-cultural message. We admire antiheroes like Holden Caulfield in *Catcher in the Rye,* Randle McMurphy in *One Flew Over the Cuckoo's Nest,* or Don Draper in *Mad Men*—outsiders who lurk at the margins, test the system. We honor trailblazers like Hildegard of Bingen, Eleanor Roosevelt, Dorothy Day, and others who refused the boundaries of traditional roles. But in their own way, those women were listeners too—hearers of a different song.

Most people in religious life have a story or two about the test of obedience. Usually it involves a seemingly insensitive superior who requires them to detour from a plan they had laid out for themselves. In her memoir *Scarred by Struggle, Transformed by Hope,* the Benedictine sister and spiritual teacher Joan Chittister tells of being accepted to a Masters in Fine Arts creative writing program at Iowa State University. At the time, she was teaching high school English, but dreamed of writing the kind of literature she was presenting in class. The Iowa State program threw her a lifeline. She recalls how after she received her acceptance letter, "Every day was suddenly easier than it had ever been before. Every moment was light . . . I could afford to treat the daily nature of grades and papers and class periods lovingly. There was suddenly no burden to it at all. Just finality. Just conclusion. Just gratitude."

That would all end in a single hurried conversation. In a complete reversal, her prioress at the time—the same one who encouraged her to apply to the MFA program—told her the dream of studying creative writing would have to wait. She was needed to work as a third cook (yes, third cook!) at a summer camp run by her monastery. Sister Joan needed the kitchen job, her superior said, to deepen her humility.

"And so began one of the greatest struggles in my life," Sister Joan writes. "I now wonder how I could have become the person I was meant to be if I had ever become the writer I thought Iowa State would make me."

As is often the case, we can't see beyond immediate disappointment. In the end, what seemed an insurmountable setback only deepened Sister Joan's conviction that she was meant to write. She overcame the confines of her superior's order by writing in her spare time with an even greater fervor. Having published dozens of books that have sold more than a million copies, she says she now looks back at that dark disappointment as the moment she realized no obstacle could deter her from her twin vocations, as a Benedictine and a writer.

Sister Irene Nowell of Mount St. Scholastica Monastery in Kansas is one of the world's foremost Scripture scholars. But that is not the path she envisioned for herself. She arrived at her monastery an accomplished cellist. She expected to continue her musical studies in graduate school. Instead, her prioress informed her she would have to study German. "I said, 'Mother, I don't want a degree in German,'" Sister Irene recalls.

"She said, 'That's not the right answer.' So I went off to get a degree in German."

Many years later, Sister Irene asked to study Scripture at St. John's University in Minnesota. "I got hooked on Scripture," she says. "And do you know what they said? They told me the German degree was the best preparation I could have had because at that point so much of the research on Scripture had been written in German."

Scripture—and music—became the defining themes of her life. She has written a translation of the Psalms for her community's Liturgy of the Hours and was one of the scholars who worked on the English translation of the revised Catholic Bible as well as the *St. John's Bible*, the first illuminated Bible in five hundred years, commissioned by St. John's Abbey in Minnesota.

"So what the prioress did for me in forcing me to study German was really prophetic," Sister Irene now says.

The stories of these two Benedictine women remind me that I have to listen not only to my inner voice, but to outside—and sometimes unwelcome—voices as well, like that of my colleague who warned that my strong opinions can sometimes be grating. Disappointment is often a useful teacher. Can I have the courage to listen to it, to discern where it might be leading me?

> *Let us open our eyes to the light that comes from God*
> *and our ears to the voice from the heavens that every-*
> *day calls out this charge: If you hear God's voice today,*

harden not your hearts (Ps 95:8). And again, You that
have ears to hear, listen to what the Spirit says. (Rv 2:7).
—FROM THE PROLOGUE

In listening with the ear of the heart, I've often discovered wisdom comes from what at first might seem an unlikely source. My father finished high school by attending night classes while working during the day. He earned his living as a truck driver. I, with my advanced degrees, often dismissed what he had to say. I know now that while my book learning might have given me knowledge, it didn't necessarily make me wise. My father had a staple of sayings he was fond of repeating. One of them was, "When you're hungry you eat, when you're tired, you sleep." That one used to draw some of the loudest guffaws. I guess I thought it was a stupidly self-evident statement. But there have been periods in my writing career when I have been so self-driven, I literally forgot to eat. I neglected to get enough sleep. At one point, when I was making an ample salary at one of the largest newspapers in the country, I landed in the hospital suffering from exhaustion and malnutrition—both self-inflicted wounds—and had to spend four months recuperating.

Suddenly my father's little saying didn't seem so stupid. It contained wisdom worthy of the Book of Proverbs. It's something I still need to remind myself of, daily.

I experienced a similar lesson in listening when my husband and I led a retreat one Lent in rural Semmes, Alabama. Semmes is such a small community that when I asked for directions from the pastor of the church we would be visiting, he said, "Just roll into town on the main road, pass a cotton field and the Dollar General, and you can't miss the church."

On the first night of the retreat, I arrived early at the parish hall to collate the handouts, set up the CD player, and test the projector for the opening PowerPoint presentation. I became vaguely aware of an older woman flittering around the hall, sometimes talking to herself. I remember thinking, "I'd like to talk to this woman, just not *now*. I'm busy."

I glanced over at the table I had been planning to use as a kind of altar. Someone had covered the table with a white linen cloth and placed an elaborate bronze crucifix in the center, along with a vase of fresh flowers.

"How do you like the way I fixed up the altar?" the woman said. "That crucifix there, that's been in my family for generations."

The woman I had been trying to avoid had brought the altar cloth, the flowers, and the crucifix. She not only decorated the altar, she had also brewed the coffee and baked a cake—the only cake anyone had brought to share.

I learned her name was Eva. On the second night of the retreat, Eva brought some poems she had written. One was a loving chronicle of the characters she meets on her weekly pilgrimages to the Dollar General. My husband and I thought the poem was so moving, we asked Eva to read it to the retreat group. It was early spring, and Eva talked about being an avid gardener. She said she wakes at dawn to look for new shoots beginning to break through the soil. They remind her that every day nature is renewing itself, and so are we. I soon figured out that any wisdom anyone was going to take away from the retreat wasn't going to come from my husband or me, but from Eva.

We returned home from Alabama a few days before Easter. Two cards were waiting in the mailbox. One was an Easter card from my sister. The other was from Eva.

"Hope you all have a blessed Easter," Eva wrote. "I think of you two often. Writers are like gardeners. They both grow things. When I lose someone close to me now, I don't send flowers anymore. I write a poem for the family and frame it. Poems last longer."

Who are the wise ones in our lives—like my father, like Eva? Whose words to us have been difficult to hear? Are we missing a message within the message? Are we listening with the ear of the heart?

For reflection:

:~ In his wonderful poem "I'm Going To Start Living Like A Mystic," the poet Edward Hirsch talks about walking silently, listening and observing attentively. This week, how can I consciously practice less talking, more listening?

:~ Justice Sotomayor says listening is the key to preserving relationships. How harmonious are my relationships with the people with whom I live and work? What are some of the "operator errors" in listening that have occurred between us? How can I make them right?

:~ Were there times in my life when listening deeply to a disappointment or setback, like the ones Sisters Joan and Irene suffered, helped me strike out in a new direction, or reignited a passion?

:~ What is disappointment trying to teach me today?

:~ Who are the unexpected prophets hidden in plain sight of my life? Am I paying attention to what they have to say, even if it is something I might not want to hear?

3

RUN WITH THE LIGHT

On Waking Up

Let us get up then, at long last, for the Scriptures rouse us when they say: "It is high time to arise from sleep." (Rom 13:11)

—FROM THE PROLOGUE

There is a wonderful scene in the novel *Zorba the Greek* in which Zorba tells the young foreman he's befriended about meeting a ninety-year-old man who planted an almond tree.

"What, Grandfather, planting an almond tree!" Zorba exclaims, guessing the old man won't live long enough to see the tree bear fruit.

"My son, I carry on as if I should never die," the old man says.

Zorba replies, "And I carry on as if I was going to die any minute."

"Which of us was right, boss?" Zorba asks the young foreman.

I tend to agree with Zorba. I like to think I try to live my life fully, *as if I might die any minute*. In college, I had a writing professor named James C. G. Conniff who routinely railed about students he felt were sleepwalking through life. The Jesuit writer Anthony de Mello writes, "Most people, even though they don't know it, are asleep. They're born asleep, they live asleep, they marry in their sleep, they breed children in their sleep, they die in their sleep, without every waking up. They never understand the loveliness and the beauty of this thing we call human existence." Even a long life is no guarantee that any of us will ever awaken from our emotional stupor.

That same sense of urgency to "wake up!" permeates the Benedictine *Rule*. It is especially pronounced in the early chapters. We need to get serious, St. Benedict seems to be saying, about living what the poet Mary Oliver calls our "one wild and precious life." Action verbs prevail here.

> Let us **open our eyes** to the light that comes from God . . .
> The Lord waits for us daily to **translate into action** his holy teachings . . .
> Let us **set out** on this way with the Gospel for our guide . . .
> We will never arrive unless we **run** there by doing good deeds . . .
> Are you **hastening** toward your heavenly home? . . .

And one of my favorite lines in all of The Rule:

> **Run** while you have the light of life, that the darkness of death may not overtake you.

Yearn. Love. Pray. Renounce. Respect. Live. All words that pop up early on in *The Rule*.

Most mornings, I rise around 4 A.M. to the sound of a *thwack* against our front door. It is the signature of Lauren or Junie, one of our two paper carriers, carrying out a line of work that one day soon will likely go the way of the milkman, the TV repairman, and the doctor who made house calls. Sometimes I am swift enough and awake enough to open the door and give one or the other a greeting. That never fails to startle them, accustomed as they are to seeing only dark and silent houses at that hour of the morning. I used to just scoop up the *New York Times* and dash back inside. But lately I've taken to lingering outside for a few minutes. I survey our front yard, the other houses on the block, and the sky at that moment when the birds begin their morning calls. The moon is still stationed overhead, and daylight is starting to creep onto the horizon.

I witness some strange and wonderful sights. Once it was a skunk exiting from between two bushes. It must have been a polite skunk, as I don't recall it leaving behind its traditional calling card. Often there are rabbits romping across the grass. They become quite still at my arrival, as if they are imitating statues. Other days, a snake or a slug on the front step. One morning I will never forget, I happened to look up just as a shooting star streaked across the sky. I felt so lucky to have been watching at that precise moment. I should say here that our house isn't in the middle of some prairie. It sits in the heart of a university town, so a shooting star or undomesticated animal isn't something you are likely to see. Unless, of course, you're paying attention.

On my first visit to the Abbey of Gethsemani in Kentucky, I wanted to savor the entire experience. I was determined to wake up in time for the 3:15 A.M. Vigils, the first prayers of the day. My room wasn't in the regular retreatant's quarters attached to the abbey, but rather on top of a hill overlooking the monastery in what the monks call the Family Guest House. I had to walk about five minutes down the hill to get to the abbey church. One morning I stepped outside my room before dawn and saw an amazing sight. The entire southern edge of the sky was awash in stars. I felt as if I could step inside this doorway of starlight. One of the monks, Brother Paul Quenon, told me later I had been looking into the Milky Way. He pointed to a solitary, bright star suspended in an opposite direction—the planet Venus. Suddenly the reason for waking up that early acquired a whole new dimension. The candlelit prayers in the abbey chapel and the chanting of the Psalms provide a wonderful, soulful entry to the day. So do the magical sights you can behold at that time of morning when much of the world is still asleep.

The 3rd- and 4th-century monks who lived in the desert considered the silence of the night a valuable teacher. Night reminds us that time is passing. Our lives, like days, are finite. Antony, one of the most revered of the desert monks, advised, "Each day when we arise, let's assume we won't live until nightfall. And at night, when going to sleep, let's assume we won't awaken." His wasn't a morbid fascination with death, but a reality check. We have a limited amount of days in which to live, so we might as well wake up and act now. There is important work to do.

> *If you desire true and eternal life, "keep your tongue*
> *free from vicious talk, your lips free from all deceit; turn*
> *away from evil and let peace be your quest and aim."*
> *(Ps 34 :14–15).*

> —FROM THE PROLOGUE

For Benedict, awakening our senses to our physical surroundings is the natural prelude to awakening the heart. In high school, I had a wonderful teacher for freshman English named Margaret

Henley. Miss Henley was something of an aspiring poet, as well as the faculty advisor for the school literary magazine and thus a group of us girls who fancied ourselves emerging writers. All writers, she would say, begin as observers. She challenged us one day to recall the eye color of the bus driver who took us to school that morning. I should have known this. I knew the driver's name. He was a regular along my route. He had even taped a piece of cardboard onto the corner of the bus's front window that said, scrawled in sparkle ink, "Wishing You A Good Day, Your Driver Sam." But the color of Sam's eyes? I could only guess. Blue?

Ever since that day in class, I've tried to not only notice, but also truly observe the people I pass in the street, the grocery store, or sit next to on the bus—not to mention the people I interview as a journalist. Still, I fall down on the job. As a young reporter for the *Dallas Times Herald,* I was sent to write about a man who, over the years, had portrayed Santa for something like ten thousand children. He was a jovial fellow, just about the right size for Santa, with a seemingly inexhaustible well of patience. He appeared to experience deep joy in being around children. He spoke lovingly of his own grown children.

At about eight o'clock that Christmas Eve, the phone rang at my home. It was Joe, the man who played Santa. He was in tears. He told me how much he appreciated the article I had written about him. He thanked me for being so kind to him. Because of my kindness, he wanted me to know it was all a façade. He in fact hated Christmas. His wife had divorced him. His children didn't talk to him. Every Christmas, he found himself alone. In fact, all the while he was volunteering at hospitals, stores, and children's parties as Santa, he had been living out of his car because he couldn't afford an apartment. He said it was all he could do to not think about killing himself as he took off his red Santa suit for the last time of the season.

Why hadn't I seen any of this coming? How could I, a trained observer, have missed picking up on even an inkling of this man's pain? I called my parents and told them I'd be late coming over to their home for Christmas Eve dinner. With a friend, I drove over to the part of town where Joe was sitting in his broken down car on that cold December night. We tried to convince him to come back with us to my parent's house for a meal. He didn't want to come, but thanked us for spending time with him. You could say my best gift that Christmas Eve was that I woke up.

> *What is not possible to us by nature, let us ask the Holy*
> *One to supply with the help of grace.*

—FROM THE PROLOGUE

In his autobiography, *Chronicles*, singer-songwriter Bob Dylan says one of the greatest influences on his life was his maternal grandmother. She once told him something he never forgot: "Everyone you'll ever meet is fighting a hard battle." Joe is a prime example. To truly see Joe, I first had to break out of the tomb of my own self-absorption. I had to climb out from my own battleground so I could see someone else's "hard battle."

Joe's story has a somewhat happy ending. About a year later, I ran into him. He was dressed in a business suit and said that with the help of a social service agency, he was able to scrape together enough money to begin making belts and other leather goods for sale. The business wasn't exactly booming, but he had customers among the people he met over the many years he had played Santa. St. Benedict asks us to awaken to the whisper of the sacred in our daily lives. And then he asks more. He asks that we wake up to the people around us—to truly see them. In a beautiful scene in the musical version of *The Bridges of Madison County*, the main character at one point asks her lover to look deeply at her hands, her mouth, her shoulders. She says, "talk to me, like there's something to say." One of the greatest gifts we can give to others is to let them know they are seen and heard.

The Benedictine Abbot Jerome Kodell writes about partaking of "the sacrament of the present moment." That is what I felt I was doing that Christmas Eve with Joe. It is an attitude of awareness I try to cultivate toward the people I meet every day who are fighting their hard battles. It is a way to run with the light, and live.

For Reflection:

∿ I will create a timeline of my life, noting significant events such as educational and professional achievements, births and deaths of loved ones, marriages, even traumas. Is there a pattern that emerges? Were there times when I felt prompted to "wake up?"

∿ Where does my life seem to be heading?

∿ Is my life best described by action verbs, or is it characterized by passive tense as I allow events to act on me, shaping my attitudes and responses? How can I become a more active player my life?

∿ Do I live as if I would never die, like the old almond tree planter, or do I live like Zorba—as if I could die any minute? Is there wisdom in both views?

∿ In what ways am I sleepwalking through life right now? How can I wake up?

4

IS THERE LIFE BEFORE DEATH?

On Living Fully

Day by day remind yourself that you are going to die.
—FROM CHAPTER 4, "THE TOOLS FOR GOOD WORKS"

I have always had a terrible fear of death. It often grips me in the middle of the night. At those times, I wake seized with the anxiety that I will one day no longer occupy the chair at my work desk, my place at the kitchen table, or my side of the bed.

This fear began at an early age. It may have something to do with having parents who were older when I was born. They looked like my friends' grandparents. Grandparents had the unfortunate habit of dying. I feared my parents would die and I'd be left alone.

I was also haunted early on by a sense of life's brevity. One New Year's Eve as I watched Guy Lombardo's orchestra on TV with my parents, a band member sang, "Enjoy Yourself (It's Later Than

You Think)." When he got to the line about how the years go by "as quickly as a wink!" I began to weep uncontrollably. I was four years old at the time.

No wonder, then, that when I first began reading *The Rule,* few passages leaped out at me more than *Day by day, remind yourself you are going to die.* As an adolescent, I liked characters in literature who refused to sleepwalk through life: Larry Darrell, the spiritual seeker in Somerset Maugham's *The Razor's Edge*; Eugene Gant, who yearns to leave the emotional confines of his small town and fractured family in *Look Homeward, Angel*; and of course, the insouciant Zorba the Greek. In a notebook where I kept all my favorite quotations, I dutifully copied Zorba's observation that, "All those who actually live the mysteries of life haven't the time to write, and all those who have the time, don't live them. Do you see?" Yes, I saw. I vowed to both live the mysteries *and* write.

For a time, as I focused on my writing career, I was able to put aside my fear of death, like a book I'd read and put back on its shelf. Then something happened. My mother died suddenly of a stroke. Death, my old adversary, reannounced itself as the fundamental struggle of my life. It was an adversary my life-loving mother could not overcome, and one I knew no measure of my own will could vanquish either.

What haunted me most about my mother's death was its suddenness. How could a person who was talking, joking, and enjoying a meal of eggplant parmesan one Sunday no longer exist the next? Walking into my parents' living room for the first time after my mother's death, I was overwhelmed by the stillness. The house reeked of silence.

I wondered if her death—or any death—might be easier to cope with if there had been some warning that it was imminent.

Or is it better we don't know it's the last year, the last week, the last day, and we simply live our lives and love who we love right up to the end?

> *Hour by hour keep careful watch over all you do, aware*
> *that God's gaze is upon you wherever you may be.*
> —FROM CHAPTER 4, "THE TOOLS FOR GOOD WORKS"

Around the time my mother died, I had another extraordinary experience. I was walking in downtown Chicago when I noticed a police cordon in front of an office tower. I asked a bystander what had happened, and he told me a window had fallen out of the twenty-first floor of the building. It struck a woman who had been walking with her daughter, killing the young mother instantly—as unpredictable a death as you can imagine. Once again, death seemed like some maniacal sharp shooter, randomly picking its targets. I could not stop thinking about that woman. One minute she was walking along Wabash Avenue holding her little girl's hand, and the next barreling through to the afterlife. It reminded me of a line in "For the Anniversary of My Death" a poem by W.S. Merwin. "Every year without knowing it, we pass the date of our death."

I thought about the possibility of my own death. How I hoped it would not just show up at my door, a discourteous guest, but drop a note in the mail instead, months or weeks before, as polite company would do. I remembered a character Ben Gazzara played in an old TV drama called *Run for Your Life,* a lawyer who is told he has six months to live. He spends that time driving across the country, helping complete strangers wherever he stops to find their purpose in life. Maybe I could be like that. I hoped I would have time to tear up my journals, press the clothes in the laundry basket, finish the crossword puzzles on my nightstand, toss out my torn underpants, and apologize for decades of bad behavior before removing the robe of life.

A few years after my mother's death, when I began spending extended periods at Mount St. Scholastica Monastery, one of the first friends I made was then eighty-nine-year-old Sister Lillian Harrington. I got to know Sister Lillian very well, and felt comfortable enough with her to share my intense fear of dying. One day, I asked her if she ever thought about the moment of death. She drilled her steely blue eyes into mine and told me something I've never forgotten. "I don't think about dying," she said, "I think about living."

Living mindfully, looking beyond the obvious—these were things Sister Lillian did, along with drinking strawberry daiquiris and enjoying birthday cake just a few days before she died at the age of ninety-six.

Witnessing the dying, death, and burial of a sister at the Mount was another profound experience. The sisters confront death not begrudgingly, but rather lovingly, tenderly. Unless a sister dies suddenly, or away from the monastery, no one dies alone. The sisters keep a twenty-four hour vigil at the bedside of the dying. They call it "sitting with" the person. As a woman without children of my own and a husband who is nine years older, I sometimes wonder who will be sitting with me.

When the casket returns from the funeral home bearing a sister's body, every member of the community lines up to meet it, as a bell tolls in the monastery tower. The night before the burial is for storytelling—a time for the community to remember the sister they lost—her gifts, shortcomings, eccentricities, and all.

With one sister carrying high a crucifix, community members march behind the casket the next morning to the cemetery. They stride with purpose and abandon to the gravesite. The first time I witnessed this, I remember thinking, these must be the only truly free people in America.

I don't think that their fearlessness in the face of death comes solely from their belief in eternal life. As Sister Lillian once said to me, "We don't know what happens to us after death, we just believe." I think their equanimity comes from the confidence that each one of them has lived a meaningful life. In the same chapter of *The Rule* in which Benedict asks us to daily remind ourselves we are going to die, he also gives us a blueprint for how to live:

> *Pray for your enemies out of love for Christ. If you have*
> *a dispute with someone, make peace before the sun goes*
> *down. And finally, never lose hope in God's mercy.*
> —FROM CHAPTER 4, "THE TOOLS FOR GOOD WORKS"

These are things we probably should have been taught in kindergarten.

I once interviewed a member of the Freedom from Religion Foundation, an association of nonbelievers. She happened to be a cancer survivor. She said death is what gives meaning to life. Believing that nothing awaits us beyond this life spurs us to make the most of this life. I think she got it wrong. I believe it is life that gives meaning to death. As Joan Chittister writes, "The fundamental question for a Christian isn't whether there's life *after* death, but whether there's life *before* death."

These days, as I hurtle toward middle age, I'm inspired by the artist Candy Chang. In cities across America, Chang creates interactive art installations that consist of a chalkboard, often placed on the side of a building next to a bucket of colored chalk. Stenciled on the chalkboard is the sentence, "Before I die I want to. . . . " Chang leaves space for people passing by to fill in their response. These are some of the responses people have written:

Before I die I want to:

◻ "Straddle the international dateline."

◻ "Sing in front of millions."

◻ "Plant a tree."

And one wish that catches in my throat every time I read it:

◻ "Before I die, I want to hold him in my arms one more time."

The philosopher Steve Cave gave a talk a few years ago on National Public Radio's Ted Radio Hour. His topic was, "Why Are Human Beings Afraid To Die?" Cave spoke of his own fear of death from an early age. It sounded very similar to mine. He said he eventually discovered a new way of thinking about death that helped him with his fear.

"I find it helps to see life as being like a book," Cave said. "A book is bound by its covers . . . so our lives are bounded by birth and death." He continued by saying that the characters in a book know no horizons. They are not afraid of reaching the last chapter, because they only know the moments that make up their story. We humans who are characters in life "need not worry how long our story is, if it's a comic strip or an epic," Cave said. "The only thing that matters is that it's a good story."

The only thing that matters is that it's a good story. That is why we keep death daily before our eyes.

There is a beautiful dedication that comes at the beginning of John Steinbeck's novel *East of Eden.* Steinbeck wrote it for his editor. He likens his book to an exquisitely carved box. What he says about his box, I'd like to say about my life at the end:

"Here is your box. Nearly everything I have is in it . . . Pain and excitement are in it, and feeling good or bad, and evil thoughts and good thoughts . . . the pleasure of design and some despair . . . and the indescribable joy of creation. And on top of these are all the gratitude and love I have for you. And still the box is not full."

This is what the living do. We put everything we have into our life. And on top of it all the gratitude and love we have for one another. May our boxes never empty.

For Reflection:

∾ How do I keep death daily before my eyes?

∾ How would I finish this sentence: Before I die, I want to . . . ?

∾ How do those who have passed on remain present to me?

∾ I will write a few paragraphs or draw a portrait of someone who modeled for me how to live. I will do the same for someone who modeled how to die.

∾ I will create a mental picture of myself in my coffin, and the people at my funeral. I imagine the eulogy I would like someone to be able to deliver about me.

5

THE TOOLS FOR GOOD WORKS

On Peaceful Living

Your way of acting should be different from the world's way; the love of Christ must come before all else. You are not to act in anger or nurse a grudge. Rid your heart of all deceit. Never give a hollow greeting of peace or turn away when someone needs your love. Bind yourself to no oath lest it prove false, but speak the truth with heart and tongue.

—FROM CHAPTER 4 "THE TOOLS FOR GOOD WORKS"

We live in a world awash in fear.

My friends who live in Paris don't take the Metro anymore for fear of a terrorist attack. Others I know, who have undocumented family members living in the US, worry they will receive a phone call one day saying their relatives have been taken to an undisclosed detention center. Muslim women friends say they look around carefully when they go to the supermarket wearing a head scarf. Whenever I am in crowded place, a train station, or a theater, the thought crosses my mind that some mentally disturbed person who has been allowed to purchase a semiautomatic rifle might suddenly open fire. It is as if the toxic fumes of fear and anxiety pollute the very air we breathe.

Fortunately, when I am feeling despondent about the state of our world, I can visit my mother's ninety-plus-year-old cousins in Brooklyn. Their Dyker Heights neighborhood is a mix of longtime Italian American residents like my relatives, Chinese immigrants and their American-born children, and Egyptian newcomers drawn to the neighborhood by the presence of a Coptic Christian church.

After visiting my cousins one day, my husband and I drove to see a friend of his who lives in another Brooklyn neighborhood. We passed blocks of synagogues, Hebrew schools, and kosher groceries. Men with long beards and side curls in black fedoras and long dark coats ambled along the sidewalks. Women in maxi skirts with covered heads pushed strollers. Their young sons wore yarmulkes decorated with cartoon characters. This is Borough Park, a neighborhood where many of New York's Hasidic Jews live.

As we approached our friend's neighborhood, shop signs changed from Hebrew to a mix of Spanish and Arabic. Our friend, who is American, had worked for USAID in Egypt. He says Brooklyn reminds him of Cairo. In this mini-United Nations of a borough, diverse people manage to live peaceably day after day on a cramped piece of real estate—tinier even than that other crossroads of culture, the city of Jerusalem. In contrast, there, conflict rages daily. Looking out on Brooklyn, I thought: this is the America I love.

Just a few days after the Brooklyn trip, I met with a student from Illinois Wesleyan University who had been shadowing me for a video project on professional women in our community. She asked if I would read a favorite passage from *The Rule* for her. There was no hesitation. I turned immediately to chapter 4.

Like the Prologue, "The Tools for Good Works" dazzles with its practical wisdom. I think of it as a kind of Magna Carta for ethical living. If the Prologue is a road map, "The Tools for Good Works" is like those insets on a map that chart a particular city or metropolitan area in greater detail. This chapter provides the steps we need to attain the Prologue's broader promises of a more meaningful life.

It begins with a reminder of the Ten Commandments. I prefer the moniker given to them by Benedictine Abbot Jerome Koddell of Subiaco Monastery in Arkansas. He calls them the "Ten Words of God," meant to guide us out of emotional slavery and "show us ways to live in freedom."

> *First of all, "love God with your whole heart, your whole soul and all your strength, and love your neighbor as yourself" (Matt 22:37–39; Mark 12:30–31; Luke 10:27). Then the following: "You are not to kill, not to commit adultery; you are not to steal, nor to covet" (Rom 13:9); "you are not to bear false witness" (Matt 19:18; Mark 10:19; Luke 18:20). "You must honor everyone" (1 Pet 2:17) and "never do to another what you do not want done to yourself." (Tob 4:16; Matt 7:12; Luke 6:31)*
>
> —FROM CHAPTER 4, "THE TOOLS FOR GOOD WORKS"

Never do to another what you do not want done to yourself. That is the blueprint for peaceful living. Then, St. Benedict pushes us further.

> *You must relieve the lot of the poor, "clothe the naked, visit the sick" (Mt 25:36), and bury the dead. Go to help the troubled and console the sorrowing . . . Harbor neither hatred nor jealousy of anyone, and do nothing out of envy. Do not love quarreling, shun arrogance. Respect the elders and love the young. Pray for your enemies out of love of Christ. If you have a dispute with someone make peace before the sun goes down.*
>
> —FROM CHAPTER 4, "THE TOOLS FOR GOOD WORKS"

Benedict lays out these tools in simple, declarative sentences. What he urges might seem straightforward enough, but that doesn't mean it's easy. Interestingly, he doesn't call this chapter prescriptions for good works, or recommendations, or even commandments. He chooses the word *tools*. Tools are items you learn to use well only through practice. A carpenter spends a period of time working as a journeyman with a more experienced craftsman. Every surgeon passes through a rigorous internship and residency. Even reporters don't start out covering Congress and the White House. They hone their writing and reporting skills covering the police beat, local government, and county courts, and then move on. The difference is that it usually takes only a few years to master the tools of these professions. Wielding *The Rule's* tools requires a lifetime apprenticeship. St. Benedict acknowledges as much when he says:

Do not aspire to be called holy before you really are, but
first be holy that you may truly be called so . . .
—FROM CHAPTER 4, "THE TOOLS FOR GOOD WORKS"

In my own life, as much as I admire these tools and like to think I keep them in polished condition, the truth is that too often I misuse them or let them grow rusty. One of the great sorrows of my life is my relationship with my only brother. We were never close growing up. He is nine years older, and it seemed as if he belonged to a different generation. When I was ten, he was drafted into the army and never lived at home again. When I was in high school, he moved halfway across the country with his wife to live in Texas. When my parents retired, they moved from their home in New Jersey to Texas, at my brother's urging. I was living in Washington DC at the time. I admit I was sad and not a little piqued that my parents were selling my childhood home and had chosen to live close to my brother and not near me. Did it mean they loved him more?

A few months before my mother passed away, for reasons known only to herself, my mother asked me to handle my parents' financial affairs if anything happened to her. She put my name on the bank accounts she shared with my father so that I could help him pay bills in the event she died before him. While we were making the funeral arrangements for my mother, my brother found out that my name was on the accounts. He flew into a rage. He believed *he* should have been placed in charge. It was he, after all, who had watched over my parents for twenty-two years following their retirement. That was true. He accused me of trying to benefit from the small nest egg my parents had saved and of wanting to take over their home. That, of course, was not true.

My response was to lash out at him. How dare he accuse me of trying to steal my own parents' money? Just because he was older and the only male among my siblings, did that entitle him to be the one in charge? I let my hurt and pride bleed through the rest of our dealings as we tried to give my mother a dignified funeral. I was not yet familiar with these words from "The Tools for Good Works."

> *"Do not repay one bad turn with another" (1 Thes 5:15; 1 Pet 3:9). Do not injure anyone, but bear injuries patiently. "Love your enemies" (Mt 5:44; Luke 6:27). If people curse you, do not curse them back, but bless them instead.*
>
> —FROM CHAPTER 4, "THE TOOLS FOR GOOD WORKS"

If I had been paying attention to Benedict's tools and not my own ego, I might have empathized with my brother's feeling of being marginalized. I might have focused on all that he had done for my parents in the years they had lived near him and thanked him for it. In fact, it was he who was in the hospital room with my mother when she died. I could have done all that. In anger, I didn't.

> *If you have a dispute with anyone, make peace before the sun goes down.*

I wish I could say that time has healed these wounds. Nearly two decades have passed since my mother's death, and my brother still doesn't speak to me. I have made weak efforts to reach out, like sending an invitation to my wedding (which he declined). We managed to exchange brief condolences when we met again at my father's wake, seven years later. Every Christmas I think about sending a card or letter. Then I don't. I can read the "Tools for Good Works," I can intellectually understand them, I can even try to engrave them on my heart. But it is still no guarantee I will live them. For all of us, living with these tools requires a lifetime of practice, in which we are still likely to make mistakes no matter how hard we work at it.

As always, Benedict has a word of encouragement for spiritual bumblers like me. *Finally, never lose hope in God's mercy.* It is a reminder I don't have to be perfect. I just have to be human. And keep practicing.

> *These then are the tools of the spiritual craft. When we*
> *have used them without ceasing day and night and*
> *have returned them on judgment day, our wages will be*
> *the reward God has promised: "What eye has not seen*
> *nor ear heard, God has prepared for those who love."*
> *(1 Cor 2:9)*

—FROM CHAPTER 4, "THE TOOLS FOR GOOD WORKS"

So many of our families are fractured like mine. Our country and our world seem to be cracking further into competing groups and interests. The only constant these days is conflict. But the neighborhoods of Brooklyn show us we can be diverse without being divided. My relationship with my brother may one day heal with heavy doses of courage, kindness, and forgiveness. Like a physician's instruments of healing, the tools for good works that St. Benedict describes are there for me to pick up and use whenever I need them. It's up to me not to let them sit inside a desk drawer and rust.

For Reflection:

:~ St. Benedict lists a number of tools in his chapter on good works. Among them are "relieve the lot of the poor, clothe the naked, visit the sick, help the troubled, and console the sorrowing." Have I used any of these tools recently? What was the experience like?

:~ Many parts of this chapter deal with how to respond when we are injured by another emotionally. "Do not repay one bad turn with another," *The Rule* says. "If people curse you, do not curse them back, but bless them instead." Has there been a time recently when I couldn't help but "curse back" and meet injury with injury? What did that feel like? How could I have reacted differently?

:~ Is there a family member, coworker, or friend who is difficult to love? Is there one particular experience that crystalizes the chasm between us? I will write a poem or short reflection describing the experience. What does it tell me about how we can move forward in this relationship?

:~ Benedict suggests a number of other tools for good works in chapter 4 of *The Rule*, including not nursing a grudge, grumbling, or speaking ill of another. Also these: refraining from too much eating, sleeping, or laziness. Is there one of those items I would like to work on in the coming months?

6

RESTRAINT OF SPEECH

On Silence

*There are times when even good words are to be left
unsaid out of esteem for silence.*

—FROM CHAPTER 6, "RESTRAINT OF SPEECH"

When you arrive at grounds of the Abbey of Gethsemani outside of Louisville, Kentucky, you pass an old graveyard on the way to the abbey church. You enter the cloister through an arched gate inscribed with the words, "God Alone." There is a lonely, palpable quiet. The only sounds are the thrum of insects, the occasional whine of a distant car, and the rustle of wind through the leaves of a gingko tree that anchors the monastery's courtyard.

I like to imagine how deeply this quiet must have impressed the young Thomas Merton, who arrived in 1941, a refugee from a world at war. He had left behind the artistic cauldron of New York's Greenwich Village and the intellectual swirl of an academic career at St. Bonaventure University. Merton later distilled the experience in these lines from a poem he wrote called, "In Silence."

> *Be still*
> *Listen to the stones of the wall.*
> *Be silent, they try*
> *to speak your*
> *name.*
> *Listen*
> *to the living walls.*
> *Who are you?*
> *Who*
> *are you? Whose*
> *silence are you?"*

Merton understood that silence serves as an echo chamber for truth found only in the heart. "Almost all activity makes me ill," he wrote after he had lived a few years at Gethsemani. "But as soon as I am alone and silent again, I sink into deep peace, recollection, and happiness." While talk may be the world's currency, in the Benedictine way of life silence is the pearl of great price.

> *Indeed, so important is silence that permission to speak*
> *should seldom be granted even to mature disciples, no*
> *matter how good or holy or constructive their talk,*
> *because it is written, "In a flood of words you will not*
> *avoid sin" (Prov 10:19); and elsewhere, "The tongue*
> *holds the key to life and death." (Prov 18:21)*
>
> —FROM CHAPTER 6, "RESTRAINT OF SPEECH"

In today's world, silence is a swiftly disappearing commodity. Even the Trappists of Gethsemani no longer observe the daylong silence that led to the invention of a monastic version of sign language. Today, their "Grand Silence" lasts only a few waking hours. It begins at 7:45 P.M. after Compline, the final prayers of the day, and ends the next morning at Lauds, around dawn.

In 1968, researchers found that it took fifteen hours of recording time to obtain a single hour of undisturbed nature sounds such as birds chirping or wind rustling through leaves, without the intrusion of a car starting up, an airplane roaring overhead or some other man-made sound. Today, with cell phone tones ubiquitous and music and movies streaming from handheld computers, it takes two thousand hours of recording to obtain that one hour of uninterrupted nature sounds.

For the earliest monastics, bread and silence were the staples of daily life. They retreated to caves and huts in barren places in search of it. Even then, they couldn't get their fill. The sayings they left behind underscore this. They saw silence and solitude as a means of fortifying the interior life. This is what Antony the Great, one of the earliest hermits, had to say:

"Just as fish die who stay too long out of water, so the monks who loiter outside their cells or pass their time with the men of the world lose the intensity of inner peace. So like a fish going towards the sea, we must hurry to reach our cell, for fear that if we delay outside we will lose our interior watchfulness."

There is a story passed down about Antony in *The Sayings of the Desert Fathers*:

Three fathers used to go and visit blessed Antony every year, and two of them used to discuss their thoughts and the salvation of their souls with him, but a third always remained silent and did not ask him anything.

After a long time, Abba Antony said to him, "You often come here to see me, but you never ask me anything."

The other replied, "It is enough for me to see you, Father."

Abba James, about whom little else is known, is reported to have once said: "We do not need words only, for at the present time there are many words among men. We need works, for this is what is required, not words which do not bear fruit."

As a journalist, I interview people every day and record our conversations for radio and TV. In my free time, I lead retreats and give presentations on my books. I talk and talk and talk. It might seem strange for someone who earns her living writing and speaking to advocate for silence. Yet it is something I increasingly crave, not only as a balm for my busy mind, but also as a safeguard in my relationships.

At Mount St. Scholastica Monastery, the sisters use a kind of check and balance for cultivating harmony in the monastery. It is one that applies equally to those of us in family life and the work world. "Before you open your mouth to speak," they say, "ask yourself three questions: Is what I am about to say true? Is it kind? Is it necessary?"

The last question is the true test. Is what I am about to say *necessary?* When I was a beginning journalist, my editors were always on the lookout in my copy for what they called "wasted words," words that merely pad a sentence, but add little or nothing to the meaning. We waste plenty of spoken words in the course of a day. We grumble about the weather. We complain about the amount of work we have, or about not having enough work. We criticize others for calling, or not calling, for being too lazy or too demanding.

> *We absolutely condemn in all places any vulgarity and gossip.*
>
> —FROM CHAPTER 6, "RESTRAINT OF SPEECH"

The Rule makes clear that what we say matters. The words we speak can color our attitude for an entire day, or for decades. "Speak no foolish chatter," St. Benedict warns in chapter 4, "The Tools for Good Works." "Do not grumble or speak ill of others." If I never speak another word of complaint, I will have already wasted enough time in my life grumbling about people I felt weren't behaving as I think they should (translation: they weren't behaving as *I* would). Complaining reminds me of something Anne Lamott once wrote about the futility of seeking revenge. "It's like drinking rat poison," she said, "and waiting for the other person to die."

The first words men and women who reside in monasteries speak at the beginning of their day are, "Lord, open my lips, and I shall proclaim your praise." It is a reminder that our words aren't meant for griping, gossiping, or criticizing, but for praise. *Is it true? Is it kind? Is it necessary?*

> *Monastics should diligently cultivate silence at all times.*
>
> —FROM CHAPTER 42 "SILENCE AFTER COMPLINE"

There are times when even *good words* are to be left unsaid, St. Benedict says, *out of esteem for silence.* I never encountered profound silence until I made my first visit to Mount St. Scholastica Monastery in Atchison. During Lent, the sisters remain silent at meals, in the hallways, even walking the grounds. I found myself noticing things that had escaped me before, when my attention had been focused on my conversation rather than my surroundings. It might be a bud on a rosebush that hadn't been there the day before. Or the quick red flash of a cardinal swinging from one tree to the next. It might be the wind's whisper through pine trees. When I turn off the car radio on a drive, I notice what is by the roadside, or inside the windows of the houses I pass. It's amazing what we see when we silence our inner and outer chatter.

So often now when I ride the bus along Michigan Avenue in Chicago, my fellow passengers are watching films or TV shows on iPads. They absorb themselves by reading emails or sending texts. Rarely does anyone even look up anymore. No chance then to observe the changing window displays at Macy's or Neiman Marcus, or take in the colored tulips in the flower boxes along the middle of the avenue, or simply engage in that most entertaining of pastimes: people watching. *Omni tempore silentio debent studere,* says the writing on a stained glass window at Mount St. Scholastica. *Omni tempore silentio debent studere,* says *The Rule.* At all times, cultivate silence.

Still, we can't all run off to a monastery or even a nature preserve every time we want to escape the ruckus of the city, the chaos of the work world, or even a living room full of rambunctious family members. In those times, I try to pause, even in the midst of the surrounding activity, to stare out the window and block out all sound and distraction. I create a mental globe of silence. Sometimes it means finding an empty room at the office to sit in, or stepping out for a short walk, or even secluding myself for a time in a dark corner of some stairwell.

When it's impossible to escape the company of others, I go to a place of solitude inside myself. I imagine sitting on a block of wood beside a fig tree on the outskirts of our family's backyard. This is the place I would go as a child to sit in silence, to write, and to daydream. The Internet, email, social media—Twitter, Facebook and the like—are all forms of white noise. They can become hungry wolves devouring our time. I try to limit the time I spend on email to certain hours of the day, the way a dieter learns to restrict the intake of sugar and carbs. I take email Sabbaths, during which I swear off email for an entire day or weekend.

Even avid social media users say they eventually require a break. "I need a breather for my personal sanity," a woman from Charlotte, North Carolina, told *USA Today.* A Google executive from Palo Alto, California, said reading his Facebook posts required "several moments of conscious relaxation" afterward. "I'm tired of expending so much mental and emotional energy," he added.

Those of us who have to navigate the shoals of the workplace and family life can take heart in the fact that even people living inside monasteries struggle with striking the right balance of silence and solitude. Thomas Merton had been living the Trappist life for many years when he wrote in his journal, as if to remind himself, "Solitude is not something you hope for in the future. Rather it is a deepening of the present, and unless you look for it in the present, you will never find it."

Some years later, even after he had gone to live alone in a hermitage on the grounds of his abbey, he wrote, "There is so much talking that goes on that is utterly useless. It is in the sky, the sea, the redwoods that you will find answers." In other words, in the silence, everything begins to connect.

I experienced that kind of connection very deeply one night as I watched a lunar eclipse from the balcony of a tall building in Chicago. The city was unusually calm and quiet as people trained their eyes on the sky. The moon looked like an amber, occluded eye whose lid drooped slowly lower, as if by hypnosis. At that surreal moment, watching a full moon grow darker by degrees, the only language that seemed to matter was silence. My Trappist friend Brother Paul Quenon often says, "When the heart is full, the tongue goes silent."

This is not to say there aren't also times for speaking up, as Sister Mary Lou Kownacki, an Erie Benedictine, peace activist, author, and good friend, likes to remind me. It remains a great stain of sin that the Catholic hierarchy kept silent for so long about the sexual assault of children and teens by its priests. We sin when we do not condemn the demonizing by our fellow citizens of an entire immigrant group, or a particular religion. We do need to speak out against efforts that degrade our environment or hurt the most vulnerable among us. Saint John Paul II, when he was pope, once told an interviewer he worried less about engaging in sins of commission than he did committing sins of omission: not being there for others when they need us and not speaking out when evil needs to stop.

I like to think of silence as orienting us toward the right direction. It is the pause between thought and action—the element that gives gravitas and greater meaning to the words we do speak. When I take time for silence and solitude, I regain the inner reserves I need to both do the work I love and also cultivate an interior life. Silence sets down a place for wisdom to find a home.

For Reflection:

:~ When was the last time I experienced silence and solitude? What was that experience like?

:~ What practices can I adopt to escape the constant chatter and distractions that swirl around me daily and draw me away from silence?

:~ A comic strip showed a man looking around him and remarking, "What a busy world! I think for the next five minutes I will do nothing." The man remains silent for the next few frames. Then he looks up and says, "Maybe I should tweet about this?" How much time do I spend on email, Facebook, Twitter, Instagram, Pinterest, and the like? What is it adding to my life? How much of it seems a waste of time? Is there a way to cut back and remain connected?

:~ How well do I apply the standard of "is it true, is it kind, is it necessary?" When was the last time I held back words out of "esteem for silence?"

:~ Is there a place I can go to in my imagination—even in a crowded airport, train station, or busy office—that will lead me to a place of silence and solitude?

7

"HAVE PATIENCE WITH ME"

On Humility

Divine Scripture calls to us saying, "Whoever exalts themselves shall be humbled and whoever humbles themselves shall be exalted." (Luke 14:11; 18:14)

—FROM CHAPTER 7, "HUMILITY"

As the youngest child in my family by many years, I often felt dismissed by my older siblings and cousins. They had several nicknames for me. "Stupid" and "pinhead" are two that come to mind. To this day, anger flares up in me like a match set to gasoline when I feel I am being disrespected.

One day, when I was working for the *Wall Street Journal's* Chicago bureau, I stepped onto a city bus and rather mindlessly flashed my monthly rider's pass. The driver apparently didn't see it. I sat down on one of the seats near the front and began to read a book. Then I heard the driver say, "Hey Miss, you didn't pay your fare." I didn't think he was referring to me, so I didn't look up.

"Hey, you," he said, now clearly glaring at me through his rear view mirror.

"Me?" I said. "Are you speaking to me?"

"Yeah, you."

I told him I had shown him my bus pass, but that perhaps he didn't see it as he was wearing sunglasses and it was rather dark inside the bus.

"No you didn't," he pressed on. I tried to pretend as if I was no longer listening and began reading my book again. I was damned if I was going to get out of my seat and show him the pass again. I felt that would be acknowledging I hadn't displayed it in the first place. The driver continued to rant about people trying to get away with riding the bus for free.

That's when the match flicked inside me. I rang the buzzer to be let off, but not before I got my shot in.

"If you knew who you were talking to, sir, you wouldn't be so rude," I said indignantly.

I don't even know what I meant by that. A well-educated, professional woman? A big time *Wall Street Journal* reporter? It was a ridiculous and inappropriate comment, not to mention a totally un-Benedictine thing to say. I like to think I'd react much differently today after years of studying *The Rule*. But at that moment, my pride and sense of wounded justice were all that mattered.

As I stepped off at my stop, a passenger called out loudly from his seat, "If you're such a big shot, how come you're riding the bus?"

So much for my ego. So much for not wanting to be humiliated. I have to laugh at myself now when I think of that episode. A little humility on my part would have gone a long way that day.

For months afterward, I wished I would encounter that driver again, so I could apologize, or at least say some kind word to him. I never saw him again.

Of all the chapters of *The Rule,* none are as long as chapter 7, on humility. Its fare isn't easy to swallow. Bookstores are filled with self-help titles suggesting how to become more assertive, successful, organized, or physically fit. More humble? Not on your life. Humility seems to fly in the face of our American identity. We are taught to be assertive, to stand on our own two feet, to rise above our struggles. Humility conjures the specter of humiliation (like my experience on the bus). Only humility isn't the same as humiliation. It derives from the Latin root, *humus,* which simply means "of the earth." We are all of this earth. As that stranger on the bus reminded me, we are all in this together, part of the great human experiment.

In her book *Humility Matters,* Mary Margaret Funk says that humility for Christians is akin to enlightenment for Buddhists, realization for Hindus, sincerity for Confucians, righteousness for Jews, surrender for Muslims, and annihilation for Sufis. St. Benedict's chapter on humility draws deeply from the wisdom of the Desert Fathers and Mothers, men and women who retreated to the Egyptian desert to seek God with a "purity of heart." They valued humility and strived mightily for it. St. John Cassian, who spent time observing the desert monks, wrote, "The way one sits, stands, walks and bows all speak with more eloquence than words." He found the practice of humility a way of living from the inside out.

There is a beautiful practice at Mount St. Scholastica Monastery in Kansas, where I am an Oblate. Before community prayers begin, a chime sounds. Then, members of the community stand and bow to one another. In a country where the easy hug and quick handshake are meant to establish instant parity, the bow seems wrenched out of another time and place. It says, "I bow to what is both divine and human in you." It is hard to remain angry with a person to whom you have just bowed. How different people seem to me after I've bowed to them from across an aisle. In that instant, I recognize in them my own struggles, my own sad limitations.

Evening prayer, or Vespers, begins with the short acclamation, "Oh God, come to my assistance. Oh Lord, make haste to help me." The early monks of the desert often repeated this brief prayer when faced with a temptation. At monasteries today, we say these words standing and facing each other. Together we acknowledge our common weaknesses and need for mutual help. We remember that we can do more together than separately and alone.

In the early years of Mount St. Scholastica, there was a ritual that is now no longer in use, though I wish it still was. Whenever two sisters were assigned to work together on a task, they would first bow to one another and say in English and German (the first language of many of the early sisters), "*Um Jesu willem*, have patience with me." (As Jesus would want it, have patience with me.)

I've often wondered how much more pleasant my work day would be if, when I walked into my office at the National Public Radio affiliate each morning, I bowed to my news director, bowed to my colleagues, and they to me, and we asked each other to please have patience with our human frailties.

> *We must set up that ladder on which Jacob in a dream*
> *saw "angels descending and ascending" (Gen 28:12).*
> *Without doubt, this descent and ascent can signify only*
> *that we descend by exaltation and ascend by humility.*
>
> —FROM CHAPTER 7, "HUMILITY"

The chapter on humility isn't for the fainthearted. St. Benedict places at its core the Scripture story of Jacob's ladder, in which Jacob sees a vision in a dream of a ladder extending into the heavens. Angels descend to earth on the ladder and climb back up to heaven again. Jacob wakes, realizing he has been on holy ground the whole time, only he did not recognize it. St. Benedict imagines his own ladder of humility. He constructs it with a series of twelve planks—perhaps the earliest known "Twelve Step Program."

> *The first step of humility, then, is that we keep the "reverence of God always before our eyes" (Ps 36:2) and never forget it . . . The prophet indicates this to us, showing that our thoughts are always present to God, saying: "God searches hearts and minds." (Ps 7:10)*
>
> —FROM CHAPTER 7, "HUMILITY"

The second and third steps can register as particularly jarring in a culture that stresses individual liberty and instant gratification. They ask us to put aside our own wills at times and forgo the "satisfaction of [our] desires." The fourth step is equally challenging:

> *Under difficult, unfavorable, or even unjust conditions, our hearts quietly embrace suffering and endure it without weakening or seeking escape. For Scripture has it: "Anyone who perseveres to the end will be saved" (Matt 10:22), and again, "Be brave of heart and rely on the Lord." (Ps 27:14)*
>
> —FROM CHAPTER 7, "HUMILITY"

St. Benedict's exhortation to "embrace suffering" recalls for me a passage in one of my favorite ancient Greek plays, the tragedy

Agamemnon, written by Aeschylus long before Benedict lived. "By suffering shall we learn. Even in our sleep, pain that cannot forget falls drop by drop upon the heart, until in our own despair, against our will, wisdom comes by the awful grace of God." Suffering is usually a humbling experience. No one seeks out suffering. It rips us out of our complacency. It forces us to take a hard look at our lives. And yet, as both Aeschylus and Benedict observe, when we embrace suffering—those "difficult, unfavorable, or even unjust conditions"—we crack open a space in our hearts for change, for growth, for gaining strength, and ultimately wisdom.

The climb toward humility grows ever more difficult as the rungs of the ladder progress. Steps Five and Seven ask us to publicly admit our character flaws and personal failings. Step Six says we should be content with the lowest and most menial treatment in whatever work we do. The Twelfth Step requires us to be humble in demeanor.

> *Whether sitting, walking, or standing our heads must be bowed and our eyes cast down.*
>
> —FROM CHAPTER 7, "HUMILITY"

Really? Not exactly my idea of fun living. Who willingly wants to do drudge work? Who wants to walk with head bowed? I like to do what I feel I am best at. I want to walk observing what's going on around me. I want to soak up life, engage with other people. Are these steps prescriptions for passivity? Invitations to abuse? Is St. Benedict, who so often in *The Rule* urges us to live a full and meaningful life, suggesting we should be miserable?

I've reflected a long time on this. I've come to see that this chapter isn't so much a demand that we punish ourselves as it is a plea for moderating our behavior. It reminds us we aren't the center of the universe, that our actions have consequences for others. If a mother leaves an infant at home alone so she can party with friends, she likely will hear from the local Department of Children and Family Services and could well lose custody of her child. A father who quits a job because his work isn't fulfilling, before he finds another, puts his needs above the well-being of his family. Surgeons don't leave a patient in the middle of an operation because they're hungry and it's lunchtime. There are occasions when we simply must consider the needs of others over our own.

It's interesting that three of the twelve steps of humility have to do with speech—what we say, how we say it, and whether we say it.

> *The ninth step of humility is that we control our tongues and remain silent, not speaking unless asked a question, for Scripture warns, "In a flood of words you will not avoid sinning" (Prov 10:19) and, "A talkative person goes about aimlessly on earth" (Ps 140:12) . . . The tenth step of humility is that we are not given to ready laughter . . . The eleventh step of humility is that we speak gently and without laughter, seriously and with becoming modesty, briefly and reasonably, but without raising our voices, as it is written: "The wise are known by few words."*
>
> —FROM CHAPTER 7, "HUMILITY"

All of this is another way of saying that talk matters. I've long suffered from a quick temper of the lit fuse variety, capable of exploding on short notice. For years, I explained this away by blaming my Sicilian ancestry. I come from a long line of volatile and emotional people. Increasingly, I've noticed something about my outbursts. At first, they taste "like honey in the mouth," as the writer of the Book of Revelation puts it. Soon, these flare-ups "turn sour in the stomach." This should have been a welcome insight, but it led to another problem. I would get angry at a person or situation, and then I'd get angry at myself for blowing up in the first place. My anger was supersized.

The desert fathers and mothers were particularly wary of anger, calling it the greatest obstacle to both humility and prayer. According to St. John Cassian, who spent time with the early desert monks, one of the main purposes of living a more contemplative life is to "remove completely the dregs of wrath from the inmost depths of the soul."

When I began making regular visits to Mount St. Scholastica, I marveled at how I never saw the sisters argue with each other (at least not in front of the guests!). Disagreements seemed kept at a minimum, despite the fact that monastic communities consist of many strong personalities from diverse family backgrounds. The sisters assured me that conflicts do arise, just as in families, but that screaming and yelling are not the prescriptions for resolving them. Instead, the sisters talk things out, coming to a place of either forgiveness or acceptance.

The desert monks didn't think it realistic to rid ourselves completely of anger, either. They counseled seeking its causes, and redirecting its raw power. They recognized that anger, or any of our other temptations (overeating, jealousy, self-centeredness, laziness, depression) emerge from our thoughts and feelings. We are not our thoughts and feelings. It does little good to repress them. In fact, that often makes them rear up more strongly. We can, however, redirect them. At the instant these temptations appear, we can divert them toward other, more positive thoughts and feelings. We move away from them by turning our attention toward simple actions that result in good—cleaning off our desk, writing a letter, washing the dishes, reading a Psalm, checking in on a friend, or engaging in a short prayer such as the Prayer of St. Francis. As Mary Margaret Funk points out in *Humility Matters,* when we divert our attention away from what is fueling our anger, these "affecting little vapors dissipate like gas in the air."

I've come to realize that there are two main types of anger. One springs from the ego. It rises up when we think we aren't being respected (as in my bus experience), or when we believe others aren't behaving as we think they should, or as we would ourselves. This kind of anger imprisons us in an emotional abyss. In the *Inferno,* Dante reserved a special circle in hell for hotheads like me. He placed us in in crowded swamp, condemned to swat each another endlessly.

There is another type of anger, focused outside the self. This anger is aimed at injustices. It is the wrath Jesus expressed when he saw money-changers in the temple; that Dr. King directed at discriminatory laws; that I experience as a journalist when I write about lead poisoning in drinking water, gang violence in city neighborhoods, or wage theft by unscrupulous employers.

When I find myself slipping into ego-driven anger once again, it's time to remind myself that the source of my anger isn't outside of me. It's within. It's my own bruised self-image, acting like a child who's been denied a second helping of ice cream. Except anger isn't the ice cream. It's the arsenic. Humility becomes a lens that helps me recognize the damage my rages do to me and those around me. It compels me to feed my better angels, not the angry wolves inside me.

There are some parts of the chapter on humility that appear to have little to do with our contemporary sensibilities. Warnings against laughter strike a discordant note with much of the rest of *The Rule.* Is St. Benedict saying humor is bad? Are we to mimic the monks in Umberto Eco's novel, *The Name of the Rose,* who murder the brothers they catch laughing over an ancient text?

What St. Benedict opposes isn't laughter per se, but ridicule and sarcasm. The kind of humor that denigrates others, not the *Saturday Night Live* type humor that pokes fun at the powerful in order to underscore the foibles we all share. He is talking here about the kind of joking that wounds, that runs down others to make ourselves appear bigger and better. That kind of laughter, St. Benedict says, is the humor of "fools."

In the end, humility is about love. The love that impels us to do our part to treat others with the decency we desire for ourselves. The practice of humility doesn't mean I don't get angry anymore. It doesn't mean I don't sometimes make a sarcastic comment, or try to puff up and make myself sound more grand than I am. It simply means I am constantly working to stop myself before I descend the ladder into those kinds of destructive behaviors.

> *Through this love, all that we once performed with dread, we will now begin to observe without effort, as though naturally from habit, no longer out of fear of hell, but out of love for Christ.*

—FROM CHAPTER 7, "HUMILITY"

Sometimes we fail. Sometimes we succeed. *Um Jesu willem,* have patience with me.

For Reflection:

∾ What does it mean to be "of the earth?" How does reflecting on our common bonds change our attitude toward people we find difficult or unpleasant?

∾ Is there an incident in which I could have reacted with more humility? Is there a way to right that incident? If not, can I visualize how I would behave differently in the same circumstance today?

∾ A few years ago, the monastic community of Mount St. Scholastica decided to house and underwrite the college education for two Benedictine sisters from Tanzania. The evening the African sisters were introduced to the community, they dropped to their knees and thanked the Mount sisters for their generosity. It was a stunning expression of gratitude that might seem foreign to our American sensibilities. How would I feel if I received such a dramatic gesture? How would it feel to me to thank someone on bended knee? Who are the people I would want to kneel before, and thank?

∾ What is one flaw I would like to address in myself to foster humility? Anger? Gossiping? Ridiculing? Talking mindlessly?

∾ "Have patience with me" is a beautiful expression of humility. Have I said it to anyone recently? In what context? In what ways can I have patience with myself as well?

8

THE TIMES FOR SAYING ALLELUIA

On Prayer

We believe that the divine presence is everywhere and that "in every place the eyes of the Lord are watching the good and the wicked" (Prov 15:3). But beyond the least doubt, we should believe this to be especially true when we celebrate the divine office.

—FROM CHAPTER 19, "THE DISCIPLINE OF PSALMODY"

I have never been great at praying. I am probably the only person ever to have flunked a retreat on "Prayer in Daily Life." Like many busy people, I struggle to carve out time to meditate on a Scripture passage, much less write down my reflections on what I read. The retreat on prayer I participated in was spread out over a series of months. I found it difficult even to schedule an hour a week to connect by phone with my spiritual director to discuss my progress—or lack thereof.

One of the reasons I love staying at monasteries is that there are distinct times for prayer. They thread through the daily rhythm of life. *Ora et labora*—pray and work—is the Benedictine motto. But as Sister Anne Shepard, past prioress of Mount St. Scholastica once pointed out to me, prayer *is* the work of monasteries. Monastic prayer is often called the Liturgy of the Hours, an acknowledgment that each hour of the day is as sacred as any celebration of the liturgy of the Mass.

Another name for these prayer times is the Divine Office. The word office implies daily work. To call prayer an "office" suggests we ought to pay attention to our prayer life in the same way we faithfully carry out our work duties.

St. Benedict devotes a dozen chapters in *The Rule* to the times of prayer, type of prayer, the order in which prayers are to be prayed, and the demeanor a person is to exhibit when praying.

Let us consider, then, how we ought to sing the psalms in
such a way that our minds are in harmony with our voices.
—FROM CHAPTER 19, "THE DISCIPLINE OF PSALMODY"

At sunrise, most monasteries observe Lauds, or Morning Praise. Vespers, or Evening Prayer, falls in late afternoon when work finishes. At nightfall, Compline completes the day. Trappist monasteries follow an even more rigorous prayer schedule. Vigils, or first prayers, begin well before dawn. Terce, Sext, and None, corresponding roughly to 7:30 A.M., noon, and 2:15 P.M., offer additional opportunities to pause within the work day.

The first time I spent an extended period at the Abbey of Gethsemani in Kentucky, visiting my friend Brother Paul Quenon, I wondered if I would make it to Vigils. They begin, after all, at 3:15 A.M. But when the bells rang at 2:45 A.M., waking the monks and inviting them to prepare for prayer, I bolted out of bed and started on the fairly long walk down a hill from the guest house to the monastery church. There to illuminate the path was a full moon, and in the southern sky, a swath of stars like a carpet of white Christmas lights. The Milky Way. Waking at that hour, surrounded so vividly by the vast mystery of the cosmos, I felt as though I was living the words of the Psalmist.

When I see the heavens, the work of your fingers,
the moon and the stars which you arranged,
what are human beings that you keep them in mind,
mortal creatures that you care for them? (Psalm 8)

There is something deeply humbling about interrupting our sleep to stand with others in prayer. We become part of something larger than ourselves. We realize we are a small part of the universe, not the center of it.

Sadly, I don't have the luxury of regularly stopping for prayer in the normal course of my day. Like most of us, I can't live full-time in a monastery. But I know I need a daily rhythm to live in a more intentional way. The experience of the early desert monastics offers some comfort. Ensconced in huts or grottos without benefit of clocks or calendars, they didn't follow the official liturgical seasons. They didn't know if it was Lent or Ordinary Time. They probably didn't even know if it was a routine Wednesday or Easter Sunday. Nor did they find it necessary to build glittering buildings in which to pray. How then, did they do it? They wove their baskets and prayed. They ate their dinner and prayed. They meditated and prayed. They read Scripture and prayed. They went to bed and prayed. And in the silence of their hearts, they prayed.

In his fascinating book, *The Day to Day Life of the Desert Fathers in Fourth Century Egypt*, Lucien Regnault notes that prayer isn't mentioned specifically in many written accounts of the lives of desert monks. That's because it was "part of the hidden, intimate, and personal activities" of the monk's routine life. "It was the exception to find a monk who only prayed and did no work." Now that's a prayer life I find well worth aspiring to.

As I have noted already, I suffer from a dual diagnosis: work-aholism and over-achieverism. I find hope and comfort in this ancient idea that prayer can weave through the fabric of my work life, where I spend the bulk of my time and energy. When I look upon my work as a form of prayer, I am less tempted to argue with my colleagues. I don't complain about the people I interview when I think they are being less than forthright. I better manage my temper, my need to criticize, and my impulse to gossip.

Because my work life is an endless stream of distractions and demands, taking short pauses during the course of my day has become my way of practicing a personal Liturgy of the Hours. One simple discipline I've adopted is to write a daily three-line poem—a Japanese haiku. The haiku is an ancient poetic form of seventeen syllables written in succeeding lines of five, seven and five syllables. They usually refer to a season in nature. Contemporary haiku diverge widely from this norm. Someone once composed a haiku of just one word: "Tundra." Sometimes a haiku writer will offer the bare essentials of an experience to leave his or her observation open to a wide range of interpretations, as in this sparse haiku by the 18th century Japanese poet Chiyo-Ni:

> *rouged lips*
> *forgotten—*
> *clear spring water.*

Writing a daily haiku is a contemplative practice I learned from Brother Paul of Gethsemani Abbey. "In meditation I aim for a simple awareness of the present moment," he once told me. "My haiku is an articulation of the gift of that moment, a brief conclusion to time spent in silence."

What's more important than the number of lines or the syllable count is what a haiku reflects—a moment in stasis, an experience frozen in time. It's why writing haiku is such good practice for pausing. It allows me to take my contemplative pauses where I find them. Throughout the day, I pay conscious attention to what I see and hear, whether I'm walking in the street or sitting at my writing desk. I'm on the lookout for what will become my three lines of the day. Writing those three lines turns into prayer. It gives me a greater sense of having *lived* my day.

In her book, *Seven Sacred Pauses,* the Benedictine writer Macrina Wiederkehr suggests our pauses can be as brief as stopping to observe a bird or a flowerbed, or as simple as breathing attentively. "Breathe in gratitude and compassion for yourself," she writes. "Breathe out love and encouragement for your coworkers, friends, family members . . . Your pause may be an awakening stretch or sitting quietly remembering your name."

African tribesman who lead safaris know the value of pausing. They stop often in their travels and sit quite still, listening to the beating of their hearts. They say they are trying to let their souls catch up with them on the journey. Sooner or later, we all need to let our souls catch up with the rest of our lives.

Prayer doesn't have to involve a riot of words. The early monastics considered silence the essence of prayer. In fact, "watch and pray" was a common phrase in the early church. There is a considerable amount of verbiage in today's liturgies. The words often attempt to wrap God in human dimensions, to define what is essentially mystery. When they did use words, the earliest monastics often employed short prayers that lent themselves to repetition. "Oh God come to my assistance, Oh Lord make haste to help me." Or the well-known Jesus prayer, "Jesus, son of God, have mercy on me, a sinner."

> *Prayer should therefore be short and pure, unless perhaps*
> *it is prolonged under the inspiration of divine grace.*
> —FROM CHAPTER 20, "REVERENCE IN PRAYER"

St. Benedict placed another type of poetry—the Psalms—at the core of community life. Their general brevity and poetic constructs—frequent alliteration, repetition, parallel ideas—allowed monks who lived before the printing press to easily commit their words to memory. Even after their long journey from Hebrew, to Greek, to Latin, to the myriad English and vernacular translations that exist today, the Psalms retain their original musicality. In fact, one of the greatest pleasures of being in a monastic setting is to hear the almost otherworldly sound of Psalms sung in the free-flowing cascade of a community's many voices.

> *The full complement of one hundred and fifty Psalms is*
> *by all means carefully maintained every week, and . . .*
> *the series begins anew each Sunday.*
> —FROM CHAPTER 18, "THE ORDER OF PSALMODY"

At the age of seventy-five, my friend Brother Paul is a trim, energetic man who walks four miles a day, still climbs trees, and has never undergone surgery or suffered a major illness. I asked him to what he attributes his extraordinarily good health. He credits singing a dozen or more Psalms daily at his monastery's

Liturgy of the Hours. Singing, he says, exercises the lungs and increases our stamina. Singing makes us happy.

Whenever I'm bumbling along, seeking a more sustained period of prayer, I often turn to reading the Psalms. The spiritual writer Pascal Botz describes the Psalms as "runways to God." They serve as an ancient point of departure, lifting our contemporary souls toward deeper insight. The Psalms never go out of style, because the human experiences they describe don't change.

People have prayed the Psalms in Nazi concentration camps, in Soviet gulags, and amid the smoldering, crushed metal of the fallen World Trade Center towers in New York. These prayers not only join us with others throughout the world, they connect us with all those who have ever prayed these words, and all those who ever will pray them in the future. They position us on a continuum of time where there is a beginning, but no end.

Because the Psalms were written largely in a time of conflict and exile, the harsh, unforgiving language in some of them can put off new, and even regular, readers.

> *You will shatter the jaws of all my foes*
> *you will break the teeth of the wicked. (Psalm 3)*

> *Make them wither like grass*
> *Let them dissolve like a small snail that oozes away,*
> *like an untimely birth that never sees the sun. (Psalm 58)*

> *My tears have become my bread,*
> *by day, by night (Psalm 42)*

> *My one companion is darkness (Psalm 88)*

There are people today on every continent who live with the constant threat of violence. People whose water is tears, whose companion is darkness. They understand well the impulse from which these Psalms of lament come. When we speak or read these ancient expressions of grief, we join ourselves to the pain felt by others in many parts of today's world.

And yet, there are also beautifully lyrical passages in the Psalms that have given solace to people throughout the ages.

> *You will not fear the terror of the night*
> *Nor the arrow that flies by day*
> *Nor the plague that prowls in the darkness*
> *Nor the scourge that lays waste at noon . . . (Psalm 91)*

> *Lord, you search me and you know me*
> *You yourself know my resting and my rising*
> *You discern my thoughts from afar*
> *You mark when I walk or I lie down*
> *You know all my ways through and through . . .*
> *(Psalm 139)*

And of course, some of most familiar lines ever penned:

> *The Lord is my shepherd*
> *There is nothing I shall want,*
> *Fresh and green are the pastures*
> *Where he gives me repose*
> *Near restful waters he leads me,*
> *My cup is overflowing . . . (Psalm 23)*

There is a beautiful panel in the illuminated St. John's Bible, commissioned by St. John's Abbey in Minnesota. In it, a line of gold musical notes crosses the page, corresponding to the Psalm tones that accompany the sung versions of the monastic Liturgy of the Hours. The notes run to the edge of the page, as if they are hastening through time to timelessness. In the background is a graph that represents the actual sound waves produced by voices singing in a monastic community. It too runs off the page. It is as if the Psalms are a heart that never stops beating, that pulses with blood, that never ages. I can't help but think of the word *hesed*, which appears multiple times in the Hebrew Psalms. It connotes a kind of mother love, an extravagant love, a lasting love, a love pulsing in the gut, filling the bones. That, to me, is the gift of the Psalms.

Along with the Psalms, Benedict wanted his communities to pray the *Our Father* at least twice daily. Why? With about as many lines as a sonnet, this prayer attributed to Jesus encapsulates not only our basic human needs, but the capacity we have for compassion that distinguishes us from all other creatures. *Give us this day our daily bread . . . Forgive us our trespasses as we forgive those who trespass against us.*

> *Lauds and Vespers must never pass by without the superior's reciting the entire Lord's Prayer at the end for all to hear, because thorns of contention are likely to spring up. Thus warned by the pledge they make to one another by the very words of this prayer: "Forgive us as we forgive" (Matt 6:12), they may cleanse themselves of this kind of vice.*
>
> —FROM CHAPTER 13, "THE CELEBRATION OF LAUDS ON ORDINARY DAYS"

There is a wonderful translation of the *Our Father* from the Aramaic that I like to pray sometimes in lieu of the traditional form.

> *Abba, let our lives honor your name*
> *Let your home be with us*
> *Let your ways be our ways*
> *Let heaven and earth be as one*
> *Give us today simply the bread of tomorrow*
> *Forgive us our violences as fully*
> *As we have forgiven others theirs.*
> *Do not let us stumble; give us refuge from evil ways.*
> *Yours, O God, is the place, the power and the wonder.*
> *Peace, now and forever. Amen.*

Perhaps the only other prayer I love equally is the one attributed to St. Francis.

> *Lord, make me an instrument of your peace.*
> *Where there is hatred, let me sow love;*
> *where there is injury, pardon;*
> *where there is doubt, faith;*
> *where there is despair, hope, where there is darkness, light;*
> *where there is sadness, joy . . .*

It is a hard prayer for me to say because so often I fall short of all that it asks me to do and be.

There are prayers from other traditions I find equally challenging, and grounding. Whenever I visit my undergraduate alma mater, St. Peter's University in New Jersey, I like to attend the 5:30 A.M. morning meditation at the Zendo led by my former theology professor, Father Robert Kennedy. Father Kennedy is both a Jesuit and internationally recognized Zen *goshen*. There is one prayer I look forward to in particular called the *Gatha of Repentance*. It reminds me that while we are personally responsible for the hurts we cause, we are also heirs to the ongoing flaws of human nature—the greed, hatred, and ignorance that was there at the beginning and will be there at the end of time.

> **Gatha of Repentance**
> *All evil karma ever created by me of old*
> *on account of my beginningless greed, hatred, and ignorance*
> *born of my conduct, speech, and thought*
> *I repent of it now*

So simple, but so profound. Meister Eckhart, the great Medieval spiritual thinker, once said that if you say no other prayer, "Thank you" will suffice. The writer Anne Lamott says her prayer usually consists of just three words: *help*, *thanks*, and *wow*. Some days all I can muster are similar one-or two-word versions.

> *We must know that God regards our purity of heart and tears of compunction, not our many words.*
>
> —FROM CHAPTER 20, "REVERENCE IN PRAYER"

Sometimes the best prayers are wordless. In her beautifully written book, *Abide,* Macrina Wiederkehr describes stepping outside one crisp autumn morning just as the sun is beginning to write its name across the sky. She intends to pray, but then experiences something unexpected. "I looked around, and behold—everything was praising God through the simple act of being: the carpet of pine needles in the pine grove, the geese honking their way through the skies, the arms of the oak tree stretched out in a beautiful welcoming gesture . . . Everything in its own way was praising the Creator of heaven and earth." We all can encounter those moments of transcendent prayer, if we look for them.

Chapter 15 of *The Rule* is a short one called "The Times for Saying Alleluia." It refers to the times in the liturgical year when the monastic community finished praying a Psalm by saying "Alleluia." It's one of those functional chapters in *The Rule* that deals solely with practices in a monastery and appears at first glance to lack any application to secular life. But its title has always intrigued me. Shouldn't "the times for saying Alleluia" be every day? Alleluia! I woke up this morning to live another day. Alleluia! My husband is smiling at me from across the dining table. There is tea, toast, and apricot jam for breakfast. Alleluia! These two strong legs will do lunges and squats at exercise class later today. Alleluia!

Alleluia. Yes. A perfect one-word prayer for a challenged pray-er like me.

For Reflection:

∼ The Psalms provided a way for the ancient Israelites to make sense of their world—their victories and disappointments; the glory of nature; and the tragedy of war and subjugation. Something I've done with my Oblate group is to take a Psalm that I am familiar with and rewrite it in my own words, using events from my own life.

∼ Another way of entering more deeply into the wisdom of the Psalms is to take a news report that is particularly striking. If the news is tragic, I might write a Psalm of lament. If the news is positive, a Psalm of praise or thanksgiving.

∼ Many people have drawn strength from Thomas Merton's famous prayer in *Thoughts in Solitude*, that begins, "Oh Lord my God, I do not know where I am going . . ." There is another famous prayer by the Jesuit writer Teilhard de Chardin that begins "May the God of surprises delight me, inviting me to accept gifts not yet imagined. May the God of transformation call me, opening me to continual renewal . . ." What are the prayers that have spoken to me in deep and personal ways? Can I write my own version of them?

∼ I will take one phrase from the *Our Father* and write a short meditation on what it means to me.

∼ I will compose a personal list of "Alleluia" prayers.

9

SLEEPING WITH KNIVES

On Trust

They sleep clothed, girded with belts or cords; but they should remove their knives.

—FROM CHAPTER 22, "THE SLEEPING
ARRANGEMENTS OF MONASTICS"

I often tell people that at first glance, *The Rule* can feel like learning a foreign language. You have to work at it. Reading it is not as difficult as, say, straining through James Joyce's *Ulysses*. Not by a long shot! It is one of those texts, however, that it helps to read for the first time with the assistance of a set of reflections, like this book or one of the excellent commentaries that have been written over the years, such as Joan Chittister's *Wisdom Distilled from the Daily*, Hugh Feiss' *Essential Monastic Wisdom*, or Esther de Waal's *A Life-Giving Way*.

Certain references pertain solely to customs of St. Benedict's time and can seem downright bizarre to contemporary sensibilities.

One is the suggestion that community members who refuse repeatedly to adjust their bad behavior should face corporal punishment. It's a quick reference, and the specific type of punishment isn't spelled out. It seems clear, though, that the prescription for physical punishment is meant as a last resort. St. Benedict expends far more words describing what was probably considered a much more serious penance—excommunication—being cut loose from the community, either temporarily or permanently. Still, any reference to corporal punishment clangs in the ears of contemporary readers.

Another of the sections that can seem strange to our modern sensibilities is chapter 22, "The Sleeping Arrangements of Monastics."

> *Members are to sleep in separate beds. They receive bedding provided by the prioress or abbot, suitable to the monastic life . . . A lamp must be kept burning in the room until morning.*

> —FROM CHAPTER 22, "THE SLEEPING
> ARRANGEMENTS OF MONASTICS"

Well into the 1950s, members of monastic communities slept just that way—in large open rooms in separate beds. Curtains or screens provided a modicum of privacy. This applied to women's communities as well as men's. Some of the elderly sisters at Mount St. Scholastica in Kansas still recall that custom the way soldiers sometimes look back on their basic training, with a measure of wistfulness—and relief that it's all in the past.

Undoubtedly, St. Benedict wanted to ensure that members could keep an eye on each other in the middle of the night to preclude inappropriate behavior. Sexual activity was probably the greatest concern. But there were other behaviors too. Brother Paul Quenon of the Abbey of Gethsemani recalls how one abbot locked the refrigerators after a certain hour to prevent his monks from binging on food in the middle of the night.

Surely, too, the sleeping arrangements were a way of reinforcing the notion that within the monastery, all are equals, whether young or old, noble-born or from peasant stock.

> *The younger members should not have their beds next to*
> *each other, but interspersed among those of the elders.*
>
> —FROM CHAPTER 22, "THE SLEEPING
> ARRANGEMENTS OF MONASTICS"

St. Benedict, a keen observer of human behavior, also knew that once we turn ourselves over to sleep, we are reluctant to jump back into the work and challenges of waking life. So he asks community members to shore up each other.

> *They will quietly encourage each other, for the sleepy like*
> *to make excuses.*
>
> —FROM CHAPTER 22, "THE SLEEPING
> ARRANGEMENTS OF MONASTICS"

The line that intrigues me in this chapter is: *They should remove their knives.* Anxious people concerned about their safety might sleep with a loaded gun beside the bed. Few, I would venture to guess, sleep with a knife under the pillow. Knives, however, were common tools among the monks of St. Benedict's day. They performed manual labor—tending crops, cooking, making artifacts they sold to help support the monastic community. A knife could come in handy. Some of us who have been in the Scouts might carry a small Swiss Army knife (though air travel restrictions have made this much less common). Few law-abiding citizens, however, walk around with the kind of knives St. Benedict describes, large enough that if taken to bed they might *accidentally cut themselves in their sleep*. So what can this passage mean for us today?

The night is often a foreboding time. The writer of Psalm 63 prays to be counted and not forgotten in these hours of seeing dimly, of confronting our vulnerable places. *O God . . . I remember you upon my bed / I muse on you through the watches of the night . . . My soul clings fast to you,* he writes.

Ancient desert monks often sat up throughout the night. They understood that night is a descent into the basement of the unconscious. The knives of our various anxieties are removed from their sheaths. The psyche dissects the petty slights, angry words, and annoyances of the day just past. It stirs insecurities about the day ahead. Is it any wonder that nearly half of all Americans over the age of twelve have taken some kind of prescription sedative? How can we sleep soundly when our inner world is raging?

St. Benedict wanted Compline, the last prayers of the monastic day, to steady the community for rest. *Now Lord, let your servant go in peace. Your word has been fulfilled,* we pray during Compline. They are the words of Simeon, the Jewish elder we meet in the New Testament who believes his life is finally complete when he sees the savior of Israel. He is ready for eternal rest. At the Abbey of Gethsemani, a lovely hymn accompanies that prayer, just as the monks prepare to retire to their beds:

> *Lord save us while we are awake*
> *Protect us while we are asleep, that we may keep our*
> *watch with Christ*
> *And when we sleep*
> *Rest in his peace.*

I like to use this time before retiring to complete what the Benedictine writer Macrina Wiederkehr calls a "spiritual gleaning." A gleaner is someone who walks through fields, gathering what has been left by the reapers. At day's end, she says, "Ask yourself—does anything come together in a clearer picture? Is there anything I missed? How does this day of creation feel in my heart? Has the day been for me a deep listening, a patient waiting, a tender abiding, a loving romance, and a joyful expectation?"

The day at many monasteries ends not just with lights out, but with a sprinkling of holy water by the abbot or prioress to bless individually the members of the community and guests. It is the final image the community sees before facing the darkness and the innumerable emotional demons that night can conjure.

As someone who has trouble shutting down the mind's machinery when it's time to sleep, I wonder if it might not be worthwhile to splash a bit of holy water onto my own forehead. It's a way of acknowledging that so many things around me are beyond my control. I might as well rest in peace. St. Benedict wanted his monks to place their trust at that most vulnerable time of day in the unseen Presence. To strike an attitude, as Abbot Jerome Koddell puts it, that "God is, and I am not." I don't have to be responsible for creating, fixing, or improving everything. I can leave that to a Presence more powerful than me. What if you are not a believer, you might ask, but still are besieged by these same nighttime fears? Perhaps you can entrust your psychic knives to the universe, a place that seems (most of the time at least) to work toward the good.

Each night unfolds the promise of another beginning. When the time for sleep ends, a new day of action begins. We return the knives of our anger, anxiety, and insecurity to their holders. With a prayerful attitude, they can become once again tools for our work, and not the weapons of our fears.

For Reflection:

:~ What are the knives of anxiety I carry within me? How can I restore them to their sheaths?

:~ What do I appreciate about the nighttime?

:~ Are there some nightly practices I might follow to aid me in rest?

:~ *Now, Lord, let your servant go in peace, your word has been fulfilled* is one of the prayers said every night before the monastic community retires for sleep. Can I write a comforting prayer to say nightly before retiring to sleep?

10

LINKING ARMS

On Community

"Try to be the first to show respect to the other"
(Rom 12:10) supporting with the greatest patience one
another's weaknesses of body or behavior.

—FROM CHAPTER 72, "THE GOOD ZEAL OF MONASTICS"

Much of my life I've struggled to belong. The search for "home" led me to schools in France and Italy, to jobs in Washington DC, Chicago, and London, and brought me finally to a monastery on a hill in the heart of America's heartland. There, I found what I was looking for.

I was the youngest child in my family, born thirteen and nine years after my sister and brother, respectively. Several cousins were born around the same time as my sister and brother. They shared inside jokes, played Monopoly together, and generally operated as a unit. Then there was me—over there, always looking on, and rarely invited in.

As a career, I chose writing and journalism. Writers and journalists are observers, people lingering at the margins. A large portion of my adult life I spent as a single woman in cities where no other family members lived. In Chicago, I moved into a high rise where hundreds of other people lived. I could actually peer into the living room of the couple who lived in the building next door to mine. I saw them sit down to dinner, and could see what they were watching on TV. The buildings were that close. Yet I felt utterly alone.

I found comfort in community. During my junior year abroad, I became part of a community of international friends at the *Union Chretienne des Jeunes Filles*, a French version of the YWCA, that housed young single women working or studying in Paris. Later, a French family with a daughter my age invited me to stay in their home during my final month in Paris. When I moved to Washington, DC for my first job after college, I was fortunate enough to meet another young professional, a lawyer, whose large Lithuanian-American family welcomed me for Thanksgiving dinners and other family gatherings. In Chicago, my Italian-American professional club and the members of my parish, Immaculate Conception, celebrated my achievements, grieved my disappointments, and helped me deliberate on decisions. These communities became my surrogate family.

Still, those were often lonely years, long before I met my beautiful husband. But they taught me something valuable. While we may not have the marriage partner we desire or the family we want, we can all have community.

My friend Sister Thomasita Homan of Mount St. Scholastica once described a monastic community as "a place where people agree to link arms, support one another, and help each other grow." Of course it is much more, too, otherwise monastic life wouldn't be that much different from the Girl Scouts! But her description is nonetheless apt.

The sign-up sheet is a constant presence on monastery bulletin boards. In many of the newsrooms where I've worked, people literally tried to keep their heads down at their desks so an editor wouldn't walk by and hand them another assignment. At the Mount, when a sister asks for help—setting up for a special celebration, baking cookies, or addressing envelopes—it's usually only a matter of minutes before the volunteer slots are filled.

I saw this firsthand soon after I began spending time at the Mount. A few weeks before Christmas, a sister put a notice up asking for help pasting holiday greetings on the dozens of plates of cookies the sisters bake at Christmastime for the monastery's friends and donors. I noticed that unlike other sign-up sheets, this one didn't have the usual spaces for people to sign their names. I wondered if anyone would come. I decided to show up in case no one else did. About a half dozen sisters were already there when I arrived. The entire task of labeling about a hundred plates of cookies took some fifteen minutes. Their willingness to help one another, no matter how small or large the task, reminds me of something William James once wrote about community. "We are like islands in the sea, separate on the surface, but connected in the deep."

I've often felt that the kind of energy people expend out of obligation to family members—carting them to after-school events, washing their clothes, cooking their meals—members of a monastic community show to one another out of a shared commitment to simply love. Visitors to monasteries often remark how peaceful the atmosphere is. Perhaps that's because they don't sense the kind of tension or chaos that fills so many homes—my own included.

Home is a place where when you come, they have to take you in, Robert Frost famously wrote. But community is something you construct, small decency by small decency.

This is not an easy thing. A monastic community, after all, is a bit like my cousins' neighborhood in Brooklyn. It represents a collection of people from disparate cultures and races who must coexist in a single cauldron. There are bound to be sparks, misunderstandings, trampled feelings.

I once asked Sister Molly Brockwell of Mount St. Scholastica how conflicts get resolved there. Her response wasn't exactly what I was expecting. "What gets confusing sometimes," she said, "is that we think liking is the same thing as respecting, or loving, or caring for a person. Well, no. Liking comes and goes fast. What we aim for is a deeper relationship—one that says we're in this together, that there is something bigger going on between us. We can disagree with one another and not see that as a total betrayal or as a chance to hack the other person to pieces, or view each other as a never-ending threat."

We can disagree and not see each other as a never-ending threat.

Sister Molly tells the story of an elderly Mount sister who was experiencing the stages of dementia. She loved talking with guests and newcomers to the community, often asking, "Now who are *you*?" One day in the dining room, she sat at Sister Molly's table and asked how long she'd been at the monastery. "I told her six weeks," Sister Molly recalled. "She smiled when I said that. She had this face that just lit up when she smiled. 'You'll do fine,' she said. 'Only the nuts stay.'"

There's humor in that, but also wisdom. "We're all a little nutty," Sister Molly says. "That's what makes community."

In some ways, St. Benedict's time was not so different from our own. A proud civilization faced daily threats from violent outside forces. Power lay concentrated in the wealthy few. Faith in public officials, religious leaders, and traditional institutions had faded. Benedict saw a crumbling Roman Empire and refused to crumble with it. His first inclination was to flee—to find a nice cave and live far from the madding crowd. That he did for several years. Then a group of monks asked him to become their leader. But conflict, envy, and ultimately treachery set in. A group dissatisfied with his leadership tried to poison him at one point. He realized it wasn't enough to remove himself from the old society. He had to construct a new society.

Despite his bad experience with fellow monks, Benedict never stopped believing there is meaning in the messiness and trials of living with others. In *The Rule,* he sharply criticizes monks who live without shared values or agreed-upon rules.

> *Their law is what they like to do, whatever strikes their fancy.*
> —FROM CHAPTER 1, "THE KINDS OF MONASTICS"

He denounces in particular those known as gyrovagues (great word!) who drift from region to region, never staying in one place long enough to make a contribution.

> *Always on the move, they never settle down, and are slaves to their own wills and gross appetites.*
> —FROM CHAPTER 1, "THE KINDS OF MONASTICS"

Basil, an elder among the desert monks, was asked back in the 4th century why he chose to live in community rather than in solitude. The word monastic, after all, derives from *monos*, meaning one. One who forgoes a spouse and family. One who seeks God with single-minded devotion. Couldn't Basil seek God more purposefully if he lived on his own as a hermit? Yes, the old monk responded. He could probably seek holiness with single-minded purpose by living alone in the desert. "But then," he asked, "whose feet would I wash?"

The call to community is tied closely to the Benedictine value of constancy. Alone among religious orders, Benedictines take a vow of stability. They promise to remain within the same monastery for life. In Western culture, staying in place is a largely foreign concept. Moving connotes upward mobility; remaining in place, stagnation. Few people are like my mother, who lived nearly all of her life in the house she grew up in. As someone who has lived in six US cities and three European countries in the course of my studies and career, I can attest to the difficulty of remaining in place. Benedictine stability, however, involves more than a physical location—the place we hang our coats at the end of the day. It is about being faithful to our daily responsibility to care for one another. As the Benedictine retreat leader Karen Joseph points out, it is about "staying at the table." In that way, we can build community wherever we may be.

> *One born free is not to be given higher rank than one*
> *born a slave who becomes a monastic . . . Only in this*
> *are we distinguished . . . if we are found better than oth-*
> *ers in good works and humility.*
>
> —FROM CHAPTER 2, "QUALITIES OF THE PRIORESS OR ABBOT"

The monastic community is also a rare social construct where it doesn't matter if you come from the top one percent of earners, the intellectual elite, or the ranks of the under-educated and unemployed. The only rank that counts stems from seniority—the number of years you have in the monastic community. What can we learn from this? Perhaps that our real worth lies not in the enormity of our bank account, the number of our degrees or professional achievements, but rather in our accumulated acts of our service, and in how often we extend our hands and link arms with others.

There is a story in the *Dialogues of Saint Gregory the Great* that tells of a vision St. Benedict is said to have experienced just before he died. It is of the world suspended in a single ray of light. In some ways, Benedict's vision foreshadowed today's global community, where communication is instantaneous. We can watch events unfold in real time on the other side of the planet. Many of us have hundreds of Facebook "friends" and Twitter "followers" across the globe. But what does it all mean? Two-thirds of the people who ask me to "friend" them on Facebook I've never even met. As Benedictine Sister Joan Chittister once observed, "Everyone is connected to everyone else, and no one is connected to anybody."

Social media communities often provide echo chambers for hearing views that reinforce our own. This echo chamber can become a petri dish for spreading false information and half-truths. We can begin to feel threatened by anyone who doesn't look, think, worship, or speak as we do. A monastic way of living calls us to break that fear. It urges us to lean into community.

As a society, we have been growing apart for a long time. At the start of the new millennium, sociologist Robert D. Putnam wrote a book called *Bowling Alone*. Putnam found that Americans had largely abandoned group activities like bowling leagues. They stopped dropping in at the local VFW Post for a beer.

Neighborhood associations, volunteer organizations like the Shriners, and church groups like the women's Altar Society, all were dying.

Part of the change stemmed from new technology. People who once ventured out for weekly poker games could now sit alone at home and play games on their computer screen—no human partners required. Psychologists identified a new form of anti-social behavior among so-called computer addicts. As one member of a VFW Post in Berwyn, Illinois, lamented to Putnam, "Kids today just aren't joiners."

There has been a cost. These social organizations did more than build bonds among particular ethnic, religious, or professional groups. Their volunteer muscle resulted in collective projects that helped the community at large. Their members might have identified strongly with a particular group, but they remained part of the larger social tapestry, strengthening its fabric. At the same time, they acquired what Putnam calls "social capital," the kinds of relationships that make us happier, more productive people.

Putnam's conclusions, though, are not all gloom and doom. He argues that many Americans simply moved on to other types of organizations and other ways of connecting. The clever fox who encounters a lonely prince in Antoine de St. Exupery's famous fable *The Little Prince* tells us that relationships are a matter of "creating ties." We may no longer meet as often face to face, but for many people today, the virtual connections of Facebook, Skype, Twitter, Instagram, Snapchat, Pinterest, and the rest are the ways they create modern ties

Still, as St. Benedict knew, we carry within us a need for human contact. We require those joined hands that Sister Thomasita spoke of. The news reminds us of that daily. I was struck recently by the headlines from a single day. Those wounded in a terrorist attack at a California office complex can't get the rehabilitative help they need, because of cost-cutting measures in that state's workmen's compensation program. Two small girls in New York, living in substandard temporary housing for the homeless, burn to death from steam spewing from a malfunctioning radiator. In US courtrooms, a backlog of asylum seekers and those attempting to overturn deportation orders are waiting as long as fourteen years for their cases to be heard. Where is community? Where are my arms, my hands in all this?

It's easy to want to turn away from problems I alone can't solve. There is, though, something I can do to extend that sense of community and belonging I experienced the first time I stepped foot in Mount St. Scholastica. It goes back to something else Sister Molly told me. "It is really quite simple when we finally realize it," she said. "Community is about the people sitting right next to you. It's not some lofty thing we need to aspire to, it's honoring the relationships right around us."

There is a beautiful scene in a film from the 1980s called *The Year of Living Dangerously*. Actor Mel Gibson plays an Australian journalist named Guy Hamilton sent to cover the political turmoil in 1960s Indonesia. He is befriended by a sensitive, almost mystical photographer named Billy Kwan, played brilliantly by the actress Linda Hunt. Billy offers to serve as the young journalist's guide. He takes him one evening on a tour of Jakarta's slums. Guy has never seen such intense poverty. Walking through the slums of Moscow, Tolstoy had a similar reaction, Billy tells Guy. Tolstoy went home, collected the money he could find, and returned to give it to the poor.

"Yes, but that would be a drop in the ocean," Guy says.

"That's what Tolstoy concluded," Billy says. "Do you want to know what I think? I say you do what you can about the misery right in front of you. And by doing so add your light to the sum of light."

Add your light to the sum of light. To me, that is the dream—and promise—of Benedictine community. To make wherever we land a "holy city," where suffering meets solace, and the lonely encounter an outstretched hand. Community is never going to be perfect, as no marriage is perfect, and no family is perfect. The first community of Christians, the twelve apostles, makes that abundantly clear. They remained a rambunctious, competitive, duplicitous and tin-headed group right up to the Last Supper and beyond. Still, Jesus stays at the table. He keeps breaking the bread and passing the cup. We too build community by staying at the table. We add our light to the sum of light.

For Reflection:

:~ The words community and communicate share the same Latin root. They are related by root to another word, compassion, which means to "suffer with," or more loosely, to "walk beside." How do I define community?

:~ When did I last feel lonely or isolated? Perhaps it was during an illness, after a moving to a new city, or experiencing a divorce. Who are the people who stepped in to be community? Write a few short paragraphs about those people and how they helped.

:~ The people of St. Cloud, MN struggled with how to accept a rapid influx of Somali Muslim immigrants into their community. Who are the strangers in my own community? Are there some small decencies I can extend to them, to give them a sense of belonging?

:~ Can I share a meal with someone I don't know well or who is a stranger in my community, thereby adding my light to the sum of light?

:~ In what ways do Facebook, Twitter, and other forms of social media help create ties for me? How do they hinder me from forging real community? How might I use them more wisely?

11

WORKAHOLISM AND OVER-ACHIEVERISM

On Finding Balance

We hope to set down nothing harsh, nothing burdensome.
—FROM THE PROLOGUE

For nearly two years, I worked in the London bureau of the *Wall Street Journal*. I was fortunate enough to have a desk that faced a window overlooking the dome of St. Paul's Cathedral. I would arrive for work around 9 A.M., turn on the computer, and proceed to bury myself in newswires and call my various sources, hoping to scope out a story for the day. Inevitably, I would look up at some point and it would be dark. The day had passed and I'd missed it!

I was like the narrator in a little poem by A. R. Ammons, interestingly enough called "Eyesight," in which he says:

> *It was May before my*
> *attention turned*
> *to spring and*
> *my word I said*
> *to the southern slopes*
> *I've*
> *missed it.*

The poet decides to travel north to where spring is not quite so far along and he still has a chance of catching the first blush of the season. But he warns at the end of the poem:

> *It's not that way*
> *with all things, some*
> *that go are gone.*

Some that go are gone. I often say I suffer from two diseases: workaholism and over-achieverism. When I was in college, I took to heart the ancient Greek definition of success: *the use of all one's talents in the pursuit of excellence in a life affording scope.* I decided that is what my professional life would be. I was like a champion sprinter in a constant race to claim my prize. And the prizes did come. They would feel good for a week, maybe two, then I was off again, glancing in the rearview mirror at my past successes as I sped toward the next achievement, the next big award.

Friday nights would roll around and I wouldn't have any plans for the weekend, because I was too busy during the week to make them. I often forgot to request time off at the holidays, and then it would be too late to get the time to visit my family. When I worked for the *Washington Post,* I often neglected to eat or get enough rest. At one point, I had to be hospitalized for malnutrition and acute anemia—a truly ridiculous state of affairs for an otherwise healthy twenty-something woman earning a good salary. In short, I had a job that included my life, not a life that included my job.

In many ways, *The Rule* is a plea for balance. Monasteries in St. Benedict's day had to be self-supporting, and still must be today. Those who live in them have to work, and work hard. In previous eras, monasteries functioned as operating farms, growing the food they needed to nourish the community. Today, they earn income making a variety of items. The Trappist monks of New Melleray Abbey in Iowa carve caskets. The monks of The Abbey of Gethsemani make a rather famous bourbon-soaked fruit cake and varieties of fudge. The Benedictine sisters in Clyde, Missouri, sell handmade soaps, gourmet popcorn, and—believe it or not—gluten-free communion hosts.

Americans work about 1,835 hours each year, which is more than they did forty years ago when there was far less automation. Yet only about nineteen percent take their full allotment of vacation time. Fear of losing a job, but also just plain workaholism might explain why. From the beginning, St. Benedict refused to let work overwhelm. He wanted his communities to be productive. He didn't want people working until they dropped or as if little else mattered.

> *Idleness is the enemy of the soul. Therefore the community should have specified periods for manual labor as well as for prayerful reading.*
>
> —FROM CHAPTER 48, "THE DAILY MANUAL LABOR"

This line from *The Rule* is often quoted: *Idleness is the enemy of the soul.* But it is easily misunderstood. I think of idleness as the mindless piddling away of time that leads to nothing. That's not the same as leisure. Leisure—relaxation and rest—is necessary. I would go so far as to say leisure is holy. St. Benedict expends considerable time outlining the hours for work *and* rest. Kitchen servers and others who are assigned tasks can request help *so that they may serve without distress.* In a chapter called "Assignment of Impossible Tasks," Benedict says if a task proves too difficult for someone, after giving it a good effort, the worker can ask to be reassigned.

> *Should they see, however, that the weight of the burden is altogether too much for their strength, then they should choose appropriately the moment and explain patiently to the superior the reasons why they cannot perform the task.*

—FROM CHAPTER 68, "ASSIGNMENT OF IMPOSSIBLE TASKS"

How many workers today would feel comfortable telling their bosses their job is too hard? Not many, I would venture. In 2015, the *New York Times* carried a lengthy story on one of America's most successful companies, Amazon.com. Amazon managers described a practice known as "Purposeful Darwinism." It marks a way of weeding out employees who don't work fast enough or don't adapt quickly. Workers told of receiving calls from their bosses on Thanksgiving Day and Easter Sunday.

"It's as if you have the CEO of the company in bed with you at 3 A.M. breathing down your neck," one Amazon engineer told the *Times.* Employees coined a term for this type of relentless work ethic. They call it being an "Amabot," a human apparatus that aims to be as resilient and fleet as the mythological character for whom the company is named. Amazon's chief executive, Jeff Bezos, said the practices employees described to the *Times* do not represent the company's values. He called them "shockingly callous."

The Rule emphasizes that people aren't interchangeable parts. The monastery, St. Benedict says, is to offer two kinds of food at meals, so *the person who may not be able to eat one kind of food may partake of the other.* Kitchen servers receive something extra to eat before they begin work so they won't get hungry waiting on others and grow weary, or worse, begin "grumbling" about the job they have to do.

In the past, monasteries followed a vegetarian diet. That's no longer the case in most places (although increasing numbers of lay people choose vegetarian and vegan diets for health as well as ethical reasons). Even so, Benedict allows those who are sick to eat meat to build their stamina. Children and the elderly receive special portions and are allowed to eat outside of the regular meal hours when necessary. The operative doctrine in *The Rule* is "each according to need."

> *It is written: "Distribution was made as each had need"*
> *(Acts 4:35). By this we do not imply that there should be*
> *favoritism—God forbid—but rather consideration for*
> *weaknesses.*
>
> —FROM CHAPTER 34, "DISTRIBUTION
> OF GOODS ACCORDING TO NEED"

St. Benedict expresses *uneasiness* about dictating how much a person should eat or drink, noting this is a highly personal matter. As a good Italian, he accepts that he can't get community members to give up wine all together, so he says, *Let us at least agree to drink moderately and not to the point of excess for "wine makes even the wise go astray" (Sir 19:2).*

> *All things are to be done with moderation on account of the faint-hearted.*
>
> —FROM CHAPTER 48, "THE DAILY MANUAL LABOR"

Benedict built space enough in the monk's regimen of work and study for eight hours of rest. Out of these chapters emerges the Benedictine motto, *Ora et Labora.* Pray and Work. It is a call to be neither a Martha—always doing—nor a Mary—always standing by—but a synthesis of both. Action and contemplation. Work and rest. As my friend Sister Lillian Harrington of Mount St. Scholastica used to say, "If we are all Marys, we will never build the kingdom of God, and if we are all Marthas, we will never understand the kingdom of God."

In the 19th century, the French poet Charles Peguy wrote a wonderful little poem that seems to describe our workaholic culture today—and my life most days.

> *They have the courage to work. They lack*
> *the courage to be idle.*
> *They have enough virtue to work. They haven't*
> *enough virtue to be idle.*
> *To stretch out. To rest. To sleep.*

For the past several decades, multitasking has been our *de rigeur* mode of working. It has led to a lot of overworked, overwhelmed, unhappy people. Increasingly, time management experts are recognizing the importance of pausing and of working more slowly, deliberately, and intentionally. In his book *Originals,* researcher Adam Grant explores how some innovative businesses got started. Surprisingly, he discovered that entrepreneurs who pressed the pause button for a time on their start-up, to let the idea germinate in the fallow recesses of the mind, ended up creating some of the most successful new enterprises.

Grant says even when we're not working on a task, it's still active in the mind, and that's when an idea begins to incubate. Procrastination (and here I would substitute the word pausing), he adds, gives you "time to consider divergent ideas, to think in non-linear ways and make unexpected leaps."

Grant calls this practice the opposite of *déjà vu. Déjà vu* is when we think we're seeing the same thing over and over again. *Vu jade* is when we look at something we've seen many times before, and all of a sudden discover something new in it. We see it because we are looking with eyes fresh from that in-between space we use to ponder, nurture, and relax.

When was the last time we took even ten minutes to simply do nothing? Just ten minutes of no email, no texting, no Internet, no chatting, no eating, not even reading?

I remember an evening at Mount St. Scholastica when I was still tapping on my computer at eight o'clock at night. The prioress knocked on my door and invited me to have a glass of wine with her and some visiting prioresses. Stupidly, I declined and kept on working. I would like to think that faced with the same invitation today, I'd know when to quit work and enjoy a glass of wine with some interesting women. Sometimes we have to follow the sage advice of the White Rabbit in *Alice in Wonderland.* "Don't just do something, stand there."

One of the places I love to visit at Mount St. Scholastica is the vineyard. The grapevines are among the monastery's oldest residents. They date back to 1863, when the first German-born sisters arrived in Atchison from a monastic community in Minnesota. The vines are wonderful plants. They will grow and grow without much effort. But they won't produce a valuable harvest without the careful touch of the vinedresser, who has to reach in periodically and cut back the branches. Too many branches deprive the vine of the nutrients and sunlight the grapes need to grow.

There is a beautiful stained glass window in Mount St. Scholastica's choir chapel that shows a shoot emerging from the ground. The top of the shoot has been sliced off. Surrounding this image are the words of another Benedictine motto: *succesa virescit.* Cut back, it will grow stronger.

To someone like me—a recovering workaholic always enmeshed in ten projects at once, compelled to say yes to anything that's asked of me—the example of the grapevines is a reminder to periodically slow down, to survey the grapevine that is my life, and cut back on what's not essential to nourishing my soul.

What *is* essential? That's the big question. I love the final scene in a film from the 1980s called *Awakenings*. Robin Williams plays a doctor who discovers a drug regimen that can awaken a group of patients who have been locked in a postencephalitic coma. The patients have lost literally decades of their lives. Once revived, they revel in the ordinary activities of daily life: brushing their teeth, shaving, reading the newspaper, sharing a meal across the table from someone. They remind everyone at the hospital what a gift it is to simply be alive.

Eventually, the drugs wear off, and the doctor has to explain to his colleagues what went wrong. You could say the drug regimen wasn't strong enough, or the patients were too sick, he says. But out of that seeming failure, the hospital's medical professionals learned something far more valuable. It is this: that the human heart is more powerful than any drug. And that's what needs to be nourished—with work, play, friendship, family. "These are the things that matter," the doctor says. "These are the things we've forgotten. The simplest things."

Succesa virescit. Cut back, it will grow stronger.

For Reflection:

∼   What are the activities that nourish me?

∼   What are the activities I'm involved in that keep me from nourishing the soul?

∼   What must I cut back in order to grow stronger?

∼   How much rest do I get each day? How much rest should I get?

∼   I will write a work history timeline. When did I feel most fulfilled, or least fulfilled in my work? Is there something I need to change about the way I work, either at home or in the business world, so as not to slip into workaholism and over-achieverism?

12

TO MAKE AMENDS

On Forgiving

The prioress or abbot must exercise the utmost care and concern for the wayward because "it is not the healthy who need a physician, but the sick." (Mt 9:12)
—FROM CHAPTER 27, "CONCERN FOR THE EXCOMMUNICATED"

When I was a young reporter at the *Washington Post,* I wrote an article about a study a university professor had conducted on jealousy. Somehow in the course of my reporting, I mixed up the name of the university where the professor taught with that of another school with a similar name. It was a significant error, and the paper would have to print a correction. The professor I wrote about was quite understanding. What I dreaded was having to face one of the paper's best editors—a man I deeply respected—and admit that I had made such a mindless mistake.

My editor's response was hardly what I'd expected. "The mind does strange things sometimes," he said. "You made a mistake, but it's not the end of the world. Learn from it and be more careful in the future."

I walked out feeling as though I'd just been given absolution. I expected to get a lecture—a stern warning about how even a small error would erode readers' confidence in my work. Instead, I received understanding. I think if my editor had chewed me out, the lesson I learned that day would not have left such an impact. It would have been overshadowed by the embarrassment I felt at being chastised. What stayed with me was my editor's compassion. It made me determined to be more conscientious in the future. The next time, with a different editor, I might not be so lucky.

On a more profound level, my editor was extending forgiveness. Forgiveness for my human shortcomings. Mercy and forgiveness permeate Scripture. In so many stories, someone is seeking forgiveness, refusing to give it, or else offering to forgive. God pardons the fumbling, ungrateful Israelites dozens of times out of a seemingly endless wellspring of mercy. "Father, forgive them, they know not what they do," Jesus groans just before he dies on the cross. In daily life, it's hard to muster such elevated gestures of mercy. At least it is for me.

I come from a long line of hot-tempered Sicilians who've turned grudges into an art form. For decades, my father didn't speak to his younger brother, which of course meant that his third brother had to choose sides between the two of them. Growing up, I had virtually no contact with any of my cousins on my father's side. When my father finally placed a phone call to his brother—when both were in their eighties and my uncle was seriously ill—neither could recall what the original disagreement had been about.

I finally got to know my cousins after my uncle had died and when my father was in his nineties. They turned out to be magnificent people. We grieved all the lost years between us, in which we had married, and some of us had became parents, even grandparents. I remember bursting into tears as I said goodbye to my cousin Tom after we visited for the first time.

"I never knew I had such nice cousins," I said.

"We're together now, and that's what matters," Tom said.

Forgiveness.

St. Benedict devotes seven chapters in *The Rule* to what we might today call relationship repair. What is notable, first of all, is that he recognizes that even people who live in monasteries will mess up. Secondly, he exhibits remarkable patience with those who do. There is no one-strike-you're-out policy. In fact, it isn't the odd transgression that seems to concern Benedict. It is repeated patterns of bad behavior. What he condemns most loudly are those acts that disrupt the harmony of the monastery and disturb the other members of the community. Being late for prayer or work. Complaining. Grumbling. One of the most serious faults is for community members to show they *in any way despise* the vows they have committed to live by.

> *There ought to be due proportion between the seriousness of a fault and the measure of excommunication or discipline.*
>
> —FROM CHAPTER 24, "DEGREES OF EXCOMMUNICATION"

We can learn a great deal from *The Rule* about seeking and asking forgiveness, both in our families and our workplaces. In a Benedictine setting, "making amends" is more important than being sharply criticized or shown the door. Consequences apply, but there is no one-size-fits-all prescription. Someone guilty of a *less serious fault* is not allowed a leadership role at prayer, for instance. But those who are repeatedly late for prayer, who are *stubborn* or *proud* or let their grumbling infect the whole community, are excluded from both the common table and community prayer. Their penance is to eat and work alone. The severest punishment is isolation.

Even so, St. Benedict wanted the community to support those experiencing difficulty, and to not merely shun them. The *mature and wise* are to encourage *the wavering*. They should do this *under the cloak of secrecy*, not making a public spectacle of someone else's faults, or using them as an occasion to boast of one's own merits.

Repeatedly, St. Benedict refers to the abbot (or prioress) as a *physician* who is to apply the *ointment of encouragement*. If the counseling of neither the abbot nor an elder works, he says there is *an even better remedy*. The whole community is to pray for the one who is struggling *so that the Lord, who can do all things, can bring about the health of the sick*. Only after all other options are exhausted does Benedict recommend excommunication, *lest one diseased sheep infect the whole flock*. In other words, firing or demoting a worker, or cutting someone off from the family, should be a last resort.

> *(The prioress and abbot) should realize that they have undertaken care of the sick, not tyranny of the healthy.*
> —FROM CHAPTER 27, "CONCERN FOR THE EXCOMMUNICATED"

In some neighborhoods of Chicago, the city in which I reside part-time, residents live in a constant state of siege. The reason is street gangs. As one former gang member I interviewed told me, too many teens grow up without fathers, with mothers who have to work two and three jobs, and with teachers who are overwhelmed in under-staffed schools. They look to gangs to give them the security and a sense of community they crave. A stint in juvenile detention often turns a teenage gang member into a more hardened criminal. A visionary juvenile judge in Chicago named Colleen Sheehan has begun sentencing kids charged in her court not to the Cook County Juvenile Detention Center but rather to attend something called a "restorative justice circle."

Peace circles have long been part of the Quaker and Native American traditions as a means to resolve conflict. They are now integral to the growing restorative justice movement. The idea behind restorative justice is to allow people to repair the harm done, rather than merely punish them. It is an alternative way of holding people accountable. Restorative justice courts and peace circles mirror the practices for amending faults that monasteries have used for centuries.

Father Dave Kelly runs the Precious Blood Center for Reconciliation in Chicago where some of the court-ordered circles take place. The purpose is to restore relationships. As Father Kelly told me, "What is crime after all, but the breaking of relationship? Restorative justice tries to heal those relationships."

People literally sit in chairs that form a circle. The person who commits a crime and the person who has been wronged each receive an opportunity to speak and be heard. It's a process, Kelly says, that requires "radical hospitality." It begins with listening. In one circle Father Kelly arranged, a teenage boy we'll call Dante had dropped out of school and had been arrested for breaking into a home. Dante's mother was required to accompany him to the circle. Community leaders were also present.

Dante had to admit to committing the crime and apologize to the young father whose home he burglarized. Then it was the father's turn to speak. He said the worst part of the break-in wasn't that a window had been smashed and items taken from his home. What disturbed him the most was that he felt he had broken a promise he had made to his young son—that he would always protect him. As the young father told his story, it became clear he had more in common with Dante than he might have imagined. Both had fathers who were absent when they were growing up. Both were raised by mothers who often couldn't be home with them because they worked long hours to support the family.

By the time the circle concluded, the father had this request of the teenage boy: that he return to high school and graduate. He gave Dante his business card and asked the young man to check in with him. He suggested they get together to play basketball at a neighborhood court as a way of keeping in touch.

I often think of the healing my own family could experience if we could just sit in a peace circle until we talked things out. When there is conflict in the newsroom where I work, I often daydream about everyone getting a chance to say their piece without fear of repercussion, so we can all clear the air and come to some sort of consensus about how to resolve an issue.

Not all peace circles are going to end with such a dramatic a result as that of Dante and the young father whose home he burglarized. Some who commit crimes can't restore what's been taken. Some crimes seem unforgiveable. But are they?

One of the most memorable people I've interviewed is a woman named Eva Kor. As children, Eva and her twin sister Miriam were ripped from their parents and imprisoned in the Nazi death camp at Auschwitz. Her mother, father, and two older sisters all perished.

The Nazis allowed Eva and Miriam to live so they could use the girls in medical experiments. Eva and Miriam were among the children who would go down in history as "Mengele twins," experimented on by the camp's lead doctor, Josef Mengele, in a quest to unlock the secrets of genetics. Against the odds, both Eva and Miriam survived, despite being injected with various strains of bacteria.

Eva eventually married another holocaust survivor, settled in Terre Haute, Indiana, and raised a family. Miriam moved to Israel. She ultimately died of an illness probably precipitated by the camp experiments. Consumed with anger and grief, Eva decided to track down their former Nazi captors who might still be alive. Through holocaust records at the US Justice Department, she found Dr. Hans Munch, who had been at the camp but had not participated in the experiments on children. His job was to sign the death certificates of the prisoners whom the Nazis sent to the gas chambers. Munch had spent a year in prison after the war, but was ultimately acquitted at trial of war crimes.

Eva contacted Munch and asked to meet with him in Germany. To her amazement, he agreed. He had a reason of his own. He wanted to ask Eva's forgiveness. And she gave it to him. Eva later told me that it felt to her as if a sack of stones she had been carrying had been lifted from her back. "I was finally free," she said. "I was finally in charge of my own feelings."

Eva began meeting with other concentration camp survivors around the world, encouraging them to forgive their Nazi torturers. On the 50th anniversary of the camp's liberation, she led a delegation to the gates of Auschwitz. "It is time to heal our souls," she told her fellow survivors. With camera crews from across the world recording, Eva publicly declared her forgiveness of the Nazis.

Now in her eighties, Eva oversees the C.A.N.D.L.E.S. Holocaust Museum in Terre Haute. (The initials stand for Children of Auschwitz Deadly Nazi Lab Experiments Survivors). The museum's exhibits focus on children who were imprisoned or killed in the war. She speaks regularly to student groups, encouraging the young, for their own sake, to forgive those who have hurt them—whether that person is a parent or other family member, friend or fellow student.

In 2015, at the age of 81, Eva again made international news. She traveled to Germany for the trial of Oskar Groening, known as "the bookkeeper of Auschwitz." He managed the money, jewels, and other valuables taken from Jewish prisoners. Groening was on trial as an accessory to murder. Eva was there as a witness to the horrors. She soon became an emblem of forgiveness. When she approached the ninety-four-year-old wheelchair-bound defendant, he surprised Eva by reaching up to embrace her. Instead of turning away, she accepted the embrace, a moment captured in a photograph later broadcast across the world. Eva thanked Groening for admitting his part in the atrocities and for testifying to the truth of the terrors human beings had endured at Auschwitz.

Most of us would be hard-pressed to forgive on Eva's scale. There are times I think I have forgiven people for some slight or hurt I believe they caused. Then, from seemingly out of nowhere, the anger I thought I'd put to rest rises up again. That's when I have to turn again to the lessons of *The Rule* and those great early psychologists, the desert fathers and mothers. They understood anger as part of the human condition. They knew it is futile to repress those thoughts and feelings. They also recognized that we can redirect our thoughts to ones that are more positive, and to actions that are constructive. And so, "I'm angry with my sister about (fill in the blank) becomes, "My sister is basically a decent person who's shown she can be very generous, and who makes mistakes the same way I do." Or, instead of sitting there fuming about how hurt I feel, I get up and make a sauce, run the vacuum, or go for a walk.

What *The Rule* makes clear is that forgiveness is not a bolt of lightning in the night, it's a slow, steady slog through sand. It's why St. Benedict was willing to forgive several times over before asking anyone to permanently leave the monastic community. He kept the door open, not once, but three times, to anyone who left, then wanted to return. In my marriage, I've found the most powerful words aren't "I love you." They're "I'm sorry."

One of the most potent Scripture stories of forgiveness comes from Genesis. It is the story of Jacob and his brother Esau. Jacob prospers after tricking his brother out of his rightful inheritance. Esau nevertheless manages to become quite successful as well, and his grudge against his brother eventually subsides. Jacob, on the other hand, lives in fear that his brother will one day find him and try to kill him for his treachery. These two estranged brothers are destined to meet. When it happens, Jacob expects his brother to pull out a sword and slay him. Instead, his brother welcomes him. Esau has long forgotten the unpleasantness that passed between them. It was Jacob who carried the burden of that broken relationship on his back, like Eva Kor's sack of stones. He and Esau are a little like my father and uncle, who couldn't remember what had driven them apart.

In our own story, are we Esau or Jacob? Can we imitate, even in a small way, Eva Kor? Is there someone we have to write, phone, text, or email today, and make amends?

For Reflection:

~ When have I received forgiveness I wasn't expecting from a coworker or family member? What did the experience feel like?

~ How have I responded to those who came to me seeking forgiveness? Would I react in the same way, or differently, today?

~ Who are the people against whom I hold a grudge? Is there something I can do today to repair that relationship? If I am not ready to speak to that person, perhaps I can write a letter, even if it is one I ultimately choose not to send.

~ I will do a creative visualization of Eva Kor confronting her Nazi captor. I imagine what it was like for Eva to walk up to his home in Germany, to knock on the door, to see him face to face forty years after the events of the camps occurred. What would I say to the man? What would I want him to say to me? I now visualize making a similar visit to someone who has harmed me. In a similar way, I walk step by step through that experience.

13

THE GUESTS AT OUR DOOR

On Hospitality

All guests who present themselves are to be received as Christ, who said, "I was a stranger and you welcomed me." (Mt 25:35)

—FROM CHAPTER 53, "THE RECEPTION OF GUESTS"

When I was a beginning reporter at the *Washington Post*, I was assigned to report on the Washington suburbs in northern Virginia. The *Post* was my first reporting job out of college, and, until then, I had lived only in large metropolitan cities. In fact, I don't think I'd ever even stepped foot in a suburb up to that time.

I spent my first six months at the *Post* on the city staff, covering local DC news. I loved every minute of it. But I hated reporting on the suburbs. In those days, Northern Virginia was mainly a bedroom community for government bureaucrats and retired military personnel. Nothing much exciting happened. On the city staff, I had gained the confidence of my editors covering a variety of crime stories and social issues. But out in the suburbs where news was harder to ferret out, I felt my once promising career slipping away. I would often stay late at night in our cramped news bureau inside the old Alexandria courthouse, pouring over community newspapers, hoping I might uncover an interesting story.

Around seven o'clock, a man named John who was part of the maintenance staff would come by. He swept the offices and emptied the waste baskets. John was a stocky man with Coke bottle glasses who, for some reason, always wore a train engineer's striped cap. He would often hang around the office even after he finished cleaning, trying to make small talk. I found these interruptions annoying and often wished John would just move on to the next office. One night I'd just been chewed out by my editor for yet again failing to file a story. John found me sitting at my desk, literally with my head in hands.

"Hey, you look like you could use some cheering up," he said breezily. Then he burst out in full-throated singing, *Pardon me, boy, is that the Chattanooga choo choo? . . . Track twenty nine . . . Boy, you can gimme a shine . . .*

I just had to laugh. Pretty soon I was singing right along with John. *You leave the Pennsylvania Station 'bout a quarter to four . . . Read a magazine and then you're in Baltimore.*

Many years later, when I began visiting Mount St. Scholastica in Kansas, Sister Lillian Harrington shared with me a "wisdom story" she would tell when she visited schools and retreat centers. It's the story of a busy man who grows increasingly frustrated by a stranger who keeps popping up unannounced at his home . . . when he is trying to eat or do his work. The visitor never asks for anything. He says he's just dropping by to say hello. The man he keeps interrupting finally blurts out, "The trouble with Christ is, he always comes at the wrong time."

Or the right time. I realize now that the maintenance man in my office was extending hospitality. Until the day he cheered me up with his singing, I didn't have the hospitality of heart to recognize that in him, and reciprocate.

For Benedictines, hospitality isn't an abstract concept or merely a matter of etiquette. It is an integral part of spiritual life. The first time I visited Mount St. Scholastica, I felt subsumed by the warmth of the sisters. Whenever they encountered me in the hallways or dining room, they introduced themselves, asked my name, where I was from, and if I was enjoying my stay. I experienced the same hospitality whenever I went to interview any of the sisters at St. Scholastica Monastery in Chicago. There was one particular sister who was always trying to get me to eat something, whether I was hungry or not. When I visited the Benedictine community in Fort Smith, Arkansas, to lead a workshop, I left three days later feeling as though I had known those sisters all of my life. They took me around the grounds on a golf cart and let me ring the old bell that used to call the sisters to prayer—a rare treat that sent about a dozen or so of the sisters flying to the windows to see what was the racket.

It is the same whether I am visiting the sisters of Mother of God Monastery in South Dakota, Mount St. Benedict's in Pennsylvania, or St. Walburga in Germany.

Closer to home, two of my gold standards for hospitality were my Aunt Gilda and Uncle Frank. They lived in Bayonne, New

Jersey, with my grandparents in six rooms on the second floor of our two-story house. Friends continuously popped in. They crowded the small kitchen table as my uncle cooked up dishes of fried baloney and eggs—joking, laughing, talking about everything and nothing.

When I was an exchange student in France, I became close friends with a young French woman my age whose parents worked as the concierges of an apartment building near the Eiffel Tower. Rue Descamps was a fashionable street address, but Monsieur and Madame Bracque lived in a small apartment on the ground floor that doubled as the mailroom for tenants. Maman Bracque, as I called her, had once apprenticed at a Paris restaurant and loved to cook. Monsieur Bracque was a champion talker who regaled his guests with stories of his childhood in Marseille and his youth as a well-known bocce ball player. It didn't matter that they struggled to make ends meet, that their dinnerware was worn and their dining room table sat across from the tenants' mail slots. Their home was rarely without guests, sitting around that lively table, enjoying glasses of Beaujolais during long, multicourse meals lovingly cooked and beautifully presented by Maman.

I can safely say the Bracques didn't know anything about monastic spirituality. They weren't even churchgoers. But like my aunt and uncle, without knowing it, they were devout practitioners of Benedictine hospitality.

> *The prioress or abbot shall pour water on the hands of*
> *the guests, and with the entire community shall wash*
> *their feet.*

—FROM CHAPTER 53, "THE RECEPTION OF GUESTS"

Reverence for guests is a tradition that dates back to the earliest monastics. In the Egyptian desert, monks would break whatever fast they were observing to share a meal with those who visited. Monks who lived in separate cells would pool their food and gather for an *agape* meal one day of the week. Their hospitality wasn't limited to fellow monks. They gave special attention to those who weren't particularly friends, but guests nonetheless.

Monastic communities later supersized these practices. Monasteries were not only to provide the basics of food and drink and a place to wash and rest. *The Rule* said they were to show guests *proper honor.*

This was no small leap of faith in St. Benedict's time. In fact, inviting someone in could be quite dangerous. The Latin word for guest, *hospes,* can also mean stranger. It shares its root with the word *hostis,* enemy. In Benedict's day, the Roman Empire had been in a constant state of war for several years. The stranger at the monastery door could well be a marauder. That's perhaps why one of the first orders of business was for guests to pray with the community. Afterward, *The Rule* says, these visitors would be welcomed *with all the courtesy of love.* But make no mistake. Guests have responsibilities too. They are not to *make excessive demands that upset the monastery,* Benedict warns.

Counter to the conventions of the time, the poor received special attention. As a reporter, I've often noticed the deference given to celebrities, political figures, and other famous figures. Maîtres d's show them to the best tables. Restaurant owners send over complimentary food and drinks. But just let a homeless person sneak out of a store without paying for a $2.50 can of beer. Police are summoned in an instant. Benedict says you've got to turn that mindset around. It is the poor who deserve reverence. The rich, he says, get enough adulation and respect.

> *Great care and concern are to be shown in receiving poor people and pilgrims because in them more particularly Christ is received.*

—FROM CHAPTER 53, "THE RECEPTION OF GUESTS"

One of my favorite characters in *The Rule* is the person known as the monastery "porter." He is a 6th century version of a residential doorman. St. Benedict says the porter should be *a sensible old man* too feeble to roam about, but not so impaired he can't deliver a message or offer a cogent reply. And here is what I just love about the porter: he is to answer every knock with "Thanks be to God," or, "Your blessing, please." In contrast, the humorist Dorothy Parker is said to have answered her phone not with "hello" but the exclamation "What fresh hell is this?" Many days, that is exactly how I react to the ringtone on my cell phone or the little pings that let me know I have an email or a text message waiting. *What fresh hell is this?*

I love both the sentiment and the psychology of the two monastic greetings. "Thanks be to God" says you are not only open to something good emerging from this encounter, but you actually *expect* it to be a gift. If you expect something to happen, you will look for it, and more times than not, you will find it.

I appreciate even more "Your blessing, please." That's because it's the community member who asks a blessing of the stranger, and not the other way around. The porter is saying, I am no more holy than you because I live and pray within this monastic enclosure. I too need the blessing of others. We are all "of this earth."

*At the door of the monastery, place a sensible person who
knows how to take a message and deliver a reply.*
—FROM CHAPTER 66, "THE PORTER OF THE MONASTERY"

Today the strangers in our midst might be a refugee resettled
in our community from a war-torn country. It might be a person
who wears a burka, or an undocumented worker from Mexico.

A few years ago, the people of St. Cloud, Minnesota, experienced a rapid influx of refugees from war-torn Somalia. The
refugees had come there legally, sponsored by Lutheran Social
Services and other church groups. Not only were the Somali people of color in a community often dubbed "White Cloud," they
were Muslims living beside many conservative Christians. Some
residents complained that the newcomers' children were stress-
ing the local school system. The city allotted about $250,000 for
interpreters out of an overall $54 million annual budget. Locals
feared the character of their community would change. The city
rejected a Muslim community proposal to build a new mosque.
Residents even petitioned their congressman to block the arrival
of new Somalis—a move deemed unconstitutional.

Tensions reached a boiling point. At an Appleby's restaurant, a
white resident tossed a glass full of beer at an immigrant woman,
then slammed the glass into her face. One Saturday evening, a
Somali immigrant stabbed nine people at a nearby shopping mall.
The assailant reportedly first asked each victim if he or she was
Muslim. Fortunately, no one was killed. In both incidents, hate
speech spiraled into hate crimes.

I do not write to judge the people of St. Cloud. I wish I could
say for certain that the Somalis would have received better treatment in the Illinois community I call home. I don't know. I do

know the kind of hospitality *The Rule* calls us to show. It asks us to extend a hand, to bow to others, and to pray together.

> *All humility should be shown in addressing guests on arrival or departure. By a bow of the head or by a complete prostrating of the body, Christ is to be adored and welcomed in them.*
>
> —FROM CHAPTER 53, "THE RECEPTION OF GUESTS"

This is a serious challenge to anyone who wants to live *The Rule* today. Pope Francis has said that there would be no refugee crisis if every Catholic parish sponsored just one refugee family. Modeling Benedictine hospitality, he invited seven Syrian families to live in Vatican City after visiting the Middle East. When then-governor Mike Pence of Indiana declared his state would not accept Syrian refugees, Cardinal Daniel Tobin, Indianapolis's bishop at the time, personally welcomed a Syrian family to the city. Other refugee families have since followed.

In my own community, a small interfaith group has pooled funds to sponsor a Congolese family. The group had hoped to help a Syrian refugee family fleeing the civil war there, but were stymied by the long vetting process it takes for people from that country to come to the US.

One of the most heartening articles I've read in a long time chronicled the story of a newly arrived Syrian family in Lancaster, Pennsylvania, in the heart of Amish country. The Syrians were housed in a home owned by a man who had been a Vietnamese refugee. He had fled his country in the 1970s by boat. A Latino neighbor helped stock the family's refrigerator before its arrival. An Iraqi, who was once a newcomer too, served as the family's resettlement case manager. Waiting on the kitchen table was a tray of hot chicken and rice, cooked by a Syrian woman who had settled in Lancaster just seven months before. Benedictine hospitality. American hospitality.

Not everyone will have the chance to engage in such dramatic gestures of hospitality. But, to recall the words of Billy Kwan in *The Year of Living Dangerously*, we do what we can about the situation right in front of us. My good friends Gwen and David Clayborne follow the Baha'i faith. Their religion recognizes the great prophets of all the major religions and considers the founder of their faith, Baha'u'llah, to be the latest in a long line of significant spiritual messengers that includes Jesus, Buddha, and Muhammed. Baha'is stress both interfaith dialogue and interracial understanding. I was often impressed by the diversity of guests whenever David and Gwen invited me to one of their religious celebrations.

Eventually, they began hosting regular meals in their home. They invited guests of different faiths and races, people who didn't know each other well, and people Gwen and David sometimes didn't know well either.

A sign I saw years ago at a Protestant church read: *Whoever Enters Here Is A Stranger But Once.* This is what Gwen and David practiced in their home—adding their light to the sum of light.

The Benedictine way of hospitality extends in particular to those who are ill or weak. It is an idea that placed St. Benedict and the early monastics far beyond the conventional thinking of their day. In that era, the origins of most illnesses were unknown. Healthy people shunned the sick and disabled. They feared contagion, and with justification. It was also common for people to attribute an illness, deformity, or disability to some moral defect in a person's character or that of his or her parents. Benedict upended those ideas. He said we should not only respect those who are sick, but treat them *as Christ.*

> *Care of the sick must rank above and before all else so that they may truly be served as Christ, who said, "When I was sick and you visited me" (Matt 25:36) and "What you did for one of these least of my people you did for me." (Matt 24:40)*
>
> —FROM CHAPTER 36, "THE SICK"

Writing in the 19th century, Pope Leo XIII defined health care as a fundamental human right. Many Christian leaders since then have reaffirmed that belief, but it is an idea that began with 6th century monastic spirituality. St. Benedict directed monastic leaders to ensure that the ill should *suffer no neglect.* As mentioned previously in this book, there are a few jarring references in *The Rule* concerning the use of corporal punishment to discipline a community's most disruptive members. These references, while unfortunate in any age, reflect the time in which Benedict was writing. They also are at odds with the far more numerous pleas for compassion, especially toward those most vulnerable. The monastery, Benedict said, should show particular concern for children and the elderly. They can be excused from the rigors of labor. They can eat before regular meal hours and receive greater portions. Above all, they are to receive *kindly consideration.*

> *Since their lack of strength must always be taken into account, they certainly should not be required to follow the strictness of the rule with regard to food, but should be treated with kindly consideration.*
>
> —FROM CHAPTER 37, "THE ELDERLY AND THE YOUNG"

The United States is one of the only developed countries that fails to provide its citizens with universal health care. I often wonder what would have transpired if our political leaders had spent as much effort trying to improve the Affordable Care Act of 2009 as they did trying to block it and then dismantle it after it became law. What would our health-care system look like today if care of the sick was as important a value in our society as it has been for centuries in monasteries?

To this day, infirmaries and nursing care wings are an integral part of monastic communities. The Dooley Center nursing care wing of Mount St. Scholastica has consistently ranked in medical surveys among the best facilities of its kind in the country. It isn't only for the quality of medical care. What is also important is the way monasteries view the infirm and elderly. Even the most enfeebled residents of Dooley Center have a ministry proportionate with their abilities. It might be sorting the items donated to the monastery's secondhand clothes shop. It might include being named the "designated pray-er" for the guests who visit. This is the way the community says to those who are challenged: you're still valuable to us.

I remember being deeply moved by a conversation I had with the Mount's Sister Loretta Schirmer. Sister Loretta was in her late eighties when we met and confined to a wheelchair, but she still retained a regal bearing. With some amount of pride, she listed for me all of the positions she had held since entering the community: school principal, dietician, librarian. She began to weep when she mentioned her sewing. Even in her compromised state, she had forged for herself a new ministry—sewing altar cloths, hemming skirts, repairing clothing for sisters and guests. Why did she weep? "It's the one thing left that I can still do for my community," she told me. It was the way Sister Loretta continued to show hospitality.

The more I think about hospitality, the more I realize that it isn't only a matter of courtesy. It isn't only what we do for others. There is such a thing as hospitality of mind. How open am I to new ways of thinking, new ideas that knock at the door of the mind? I am sometimes surprised to discover people I know have voted for a candidate whose public policy positions I abhor. I thought I knew these people well, but apparently I didn't. My first inclination is to shove them out of my life. Just drop them as friends. But that would not be the Benedictine way. So I ask them their reasons for voting the way they did. Is there something I am missing? Benedictine hospitality calls on me to question whether I am at home enough in my own beliefs to disagree with others without feeling betrayed by them. Can I have the hospitality of heart to remember there is something larger at stake than a political position—our friendship?

As the refugee crisis around the world worsens, as diversity increases in our own communities, and as politics becomes increasingly polarized, the call to a Benedictine hospitality of mind becomes ever more essential. Rebecca Dubowe, the sole rabbi in the community where I live, often says it is far more important to ask the question, "Who are you?" than state, "This is who I am." When change comes to my family, to my community, do I respond by slamming shut the doors of my home and my mind? Or do I react to the stranger in my midst as my friends Gwen and David do, joining with Benedictines all over the world who say, "Your blessing, please," and "Thanks be to God?"

For Reflection:

:~ What does hospitality mean to me?

:~ Who are my role models for hospitality? What are my memories of them?

:~ How can I play a small role in welcoming the stranger in my midst, perhaps a refugee, an undocumented immigrant, or any newcomer?

:~ How can care of the sick become a more prominent value in my life? How can I work to ensure the sick and disabled are properly are cared for in our society as well?

:~ Is my reaction to those I meet, "Thanks be to God" and "Your blessing, please" or more like, "What fresh hell is this?" How can I become more like the monastery porter and make my home a sanctuary of hospitality?

14

DO I NEED THIS NOW?

On Living Simply

No one may presume to give, receive, or retain anything as his or her own, nothing at all—not a book, writing tablets or stylus—in short, not a single item.

—FROM CHAPTER 33, "MONASTICS AND PRIVATE OWNERSHIP"

About twice a year, I have a dream about the Oldsmobile that belonged to my parents. It is a 1992 champagne-colored Royale, a classic now. It was the last car they owned. It was also the first car in more than fifty years of marriage that they bought new. My parents always owned a car, just never a decent one. In 1972, my father was still driving the 1950 Dodge that had belonged to my grandfather. He repainted it by hand to make it look more presentable. Then came "my father's Oldsmobile," as the old TV ads used to say.

Most people have to pry the car keys away from elderly parents. Not me. My mother didn't have a driver's license, so that wasn't a problem. When she died, my ninety-year-old father threw down the Oldsmobile keys on the kitchen counter and announced he was done with driving. After living for thirteen years in downtown Chicago without an automobile, I bought the Oldsmobile from Dad. I couldn't bear to let a stranger have it. When my father died seven years later, the Oldsmobile loomed large as one of the last tangible connections to my parents. A mere whiff of the upholstery deposits me back to the times when they would pick me up from the airport on my visits home. Later, after they had both grown feebler, it was I who took them for drives in the Oldsmobile.

I've kept the Olds running in the years since my father passed away, though I no longer drive it long distances. The rubber bands and Styrofoam cups Dad kept on hand are still in the glove compartment. The New York Rose lipstick my mother wore is in the passenger door compartment. Occasionally I find some strands of ash blonde hair—Mom's preferred hair color at the end of her life. When that happens, I pick up the strands and deposit them in a plastic baggie I keep. People who see the Olds parked outside come by our back door and ask if it's for sale. I lie and tell them it's my father's car (as if he is still alive), and he doesn't want to sell it. My husband says I'll be carried out of our house before that Oldsmobile departs from our driveway.

In one of my recurring dreams, I cannot remember where I've parked the Olds. I wake in a panic. In another of the dreams, I park the Oldsmobile in an unsafe neighborhood and return to find its front window smashed and its engine stripped, except for the battery, which has been detached and is sitting on the front hood—whatever that means.

Buddhist teachers will say that attachment is the source of all suffering. They warn that all things are fleeting, as are the people we love, whom we will one day lose to death. I sometimes wonder if the Oldsmobile is an unhealthy attachment. I always conclude the same thing. It isn't the pride of owning a classic car that causes me to obsess about it. It is the memories stored in its metal hulk. It is what the Olds represents. Increasingly, though, I am beginning to recognize that just as I am not my thoughts or my feelings, the car is not my parents. Perhaps one day in the not too distant future, I might donate it to charity, or give it to someone who needs transportation. I will no longer have to hold onto it, because I will realize that I carry my parents within me.

The Rule is quite emphatic about material possessions. Community members are to share even personal gifts they receive from family or friends. This isn't because St. Benedict was an early communist. In place of private ownership, he offers an alternative. The monastery—the community—will provide for the needs of all.

> *It is written: "Distribution was made as each had need"*
> *(Acts 4:35). By this we do not imply that there should be*
> *favoritism—God forbid—but rather consideration for*
> *weaknesses.*

—FROM CHAPTER 34, "DISTRIBUTION
OF GOODS ACCORDING TO NEED"

I was once in a Verizon store getting my phone repaired when some parents walked in with a teenage daughter. She wanted the latest iPhone. Her father told her that the family couldn't afford the iPhone, but that she could choose another less expensive model.

"But *Daaad*," the young girl said, "Everyone has *this* phone."

The arguing raged on for several minutes as the daughter insisted nothing but the iPhone would do. Finally her father said, "That's it, we're leaving."

The girl didn't get her phone, at least not that day. I imagine the silence at the dinner table in the family's home that night could have frozen the Chicago River. I wonder if the girl will look back on that memory and feel sad she hadn't understood the demand she was making on her father. Or would it become a "brown stamp" as a therapist friend of mine calls the hurts we collect to prove we've been mistreated or deprived?

When I first starting visiting Mount St. Scholastica, a sister whom I did not know very well died. The night before a funeral takes place, the Atchison sisters invite "storytelling." It's a time for relatives, members of the community, and friends from the outside to share their memories of the person who died. Sister Phyllis was not a scholar, author, or sought-after retreat leader, as many of the Mount sisters are. Throughout Kansas and Missouri, she taught reading to school children. When she retired and returned to live full-time in the monastery, she requested "plain, simple work." She was put in charge of the gardens and canning fruits and vegetables. At storytelling, her cousin told of a visit home Sister Phyllis had made years before. When it was time to return to the monastery, her cousin noticed Sister Phyllis wasn't wearing her coat. The cousin asked what she'd done with it. Sister Phyllis had given her coat to the family's housekeeper.

"But, Phyllis, didn't you say you had just gotten that coat, that it was your new coat?" the cousin asked.

"That's okay," Sister Phyllis responded. "I can get another one."

The week Sister Phyllis died, two articles in the *New York Times* caught my attention. One was the obituary of Bruce Wasserstein, a Wall Street financier I remembered from my days reporting for the *Wall Street Journal.* He had engineered the kinds of mergers and acquisitions that often resulted in thousands of people losing their livelihoods. He had died suddenly of an apparent heart attack, at the age of sixty-three.

The other article was about the once-proud Simmons Mattress Company. Simmons had been acquired by a group of private investors through a buyout that saddled the company with millions of dollars in debt. To pay down the debt, the new owners laid off thousands of workers, many of whom had been with Simmons for twenty years or more—but not before the owners had paid themselves millions of dollars in fees and special dividends.

I thought about how Bruce Wasserstein and Sister Phyllis had come to the same end in the same week. How the investors at Simmons Mattress—indeed all of us—are lurching toward that same end. Not a billion dollars nor one cent can change that fact. Yet it was Sister Phyllis, a woman who never had a personal bank account, who owned no possessions but what she held in common with her community, who felt rich enough and secure enough to give away her only coat.

I've often marveled at that story, because I sometimes find it hard to give away—not just my only coat, but even one of my many coats. I once had a plaid ski jacket with white sleeves that I'd picked out with my first really serious boyfriend. I ditched the boyfriend, but kept the coat. It had gone out of style and didn't fit as well as it once had. I'd put it in a bag to donate to a parish clothes pantry, only to take it out again at the last minute. I suppose it was the memories the coat revived of a particular period in my early twenties that made it so difficult to give up. One day, I forgot to look in the donation bag before I dropped it off. I realized only after I had gotten home that the jacket had been in the pile of clothing. Instead of racing back to the parish to get the coat, I felt oddly liberated. I took comfort in imagining it keeping some other young woman cozily warm on a winter date.

> *Members must not complain about the color or coarse-*
> *ness of all these articles [of clothing], but use what is*
> *available in the vicinity at a reasonable cost . . . When-*
> *ever new clothing is received, the old should be returned*
> *at once and stored in a wardrobe for the poor.*
>
> —FROM CHAPTER 55, "CLOTHING AND FOOTWEAR"

My attachment to things is far from cured. While robbers could take almost anything they want from my home, I would guard with my life certain items because of what they represent to me. One is a tiny statue of a Native American woman seated in the middle of a circle of children, called "The Storyteller." It was a gift from the Mount's Sister Lillian Harrington, known as the "Pilgrim Minister" for her storytelling travels to schools and parishes. Sister Lillian gave it to me shortly before she died. I sensed she was trusting me to now become "The Storyteller."

Another item is an antique street brick, stamped with the name of Atchison, given to me by my friend Sister Thomasita Homan shortly after I finished writing my memoir about Mount St. Scholastica. What made the gift even more poignant was that a friend had given it to her. She was willing to part with the souvenir brick so it could delight yet another person.

I also have a small hand-carved wooden crucifix given to me on the day of my Oblation by the Mount's Sister Bettina Tobin. It too had been a gift to her, offered by a man she had met when she was a missionary in Brazil. Sister Bettina told me the poor of rural Brazil often give as gifts things that have been given to them.

Who knows the journey that cross took before it got to me? Theirs is a way of giving from the heart and not from one's bounty.

I suppose I can be accused of object idolatry by taking these gifts so to heart. I prefer to think of these possessions as sacred symbols in my life, like the stones Jacob deposited at Bethel to mark the place as holy ground. Perhaps I'm only kidding myself. Maybe in my own way, I'm perpetuating the mindset that says every person in the family needs his or her own cell phone. That every room in the house has to have a TV and every family member a separate car. This is a particularly American sickness.

I remember visiting the Thomas Merton Center at Bellarmine University in Louisville. The nearly fifty books Merton wrote in his fifty-three years of life, translated into a multitude of languages, fill several display cases at the center. Merton's personal possessions take up a single glass case. They consist of his monk's cowl, eyeglasses, work boots, and the pin that belonged to his laundry bag, still marked with the number assigned to him the day he entered. Merton's was one of the richest, most creative minds of the 20th century. He would have been a millionaire if he had been able to keep his book royalties (they went to his abbey). Still, his personal possessions amount to four items. Makes you think.

The prioress or abbot is to provide all things necessary: that is, cowl, tunic, sandals, shoes, belt, knife, stylus, needle, handkerchief and writing tablets.

—FROM CHAPTER 55, "CLOTHING AND FOOTWEAR"

It's interesting that the elderly often begin giving away the things they own as they inch closer to death. It's as if they realize the journey to what lies ahead won't require a lot of baggage. After a certain age, people begin to say, "Don't buy me anything for my birthday/Christmas/anniversary. I don't need anything." They've learned the meaning of "enough." The Mount's Sister Judith Sutera once gave me a handy saying for guarding against my materialistic instincts. Before you make a purchase, ask yourself: "Do I need this item, and do I need it now?"

Even the possessions that mean so much to me—my "Story-teller" statue, the Atchison street brick, and the wooden cross from Brazil—I will one day have to give up. I still retain the vivid memory of Catholic Charities carting away the furniture from my parents' living room as we prepared their house for sale after my mother's death. There went the couch she had covered in plastic, lest anyone spill something on it that would leave a stain. There went the coffee table we dared not set a glass on for fear it would make a mark. Out the door. Gone forever.

The social activist Edwina Gately has spent her life working with the poor and marginalized. "What we have to learn to do," she says, "is hold on to nothing." There is a passage written by the Vietnamese Buddhist monk Thich Nhat Hanh that drives home to me why I shouldn't cling too tightly to the things of this world.

> *We are of a nature to die*
> *There is no way to escape death*
> *Our actions are our only true belongings*
> *Our actions are the ground on which we stand*

Our actions are our only true belongings. The late Jesuit theologian Karl Rahner wrote, "The only thing that counts at the end of life is what we can take with us at the moment of death, which is I myself as I was in the ultimate depths of my own heart—a heart that was either full of love, or full of spite and hidden selfishness."

Wise words to keep close to the heart.

For Reflection:

:~ What are some of the possessions I feel I cannot do without? In the interest of living more simply, can I imagine myself giving them up? What would it feel like?

:~ Knowing when enough is enough seems particularly hard in America when a vast advertising and marketing apparatus exists to convince us we truly need this "one more thing." How would I define "enough" for myself?

:~ How does the question "Do I need this, and do I need this now?" apply to purchases I am thinking of making?

:~ If I were to choose not to make those purchases, what could I do with the money I save?

:~ What does Thich Nhat Hanh mean by "our actions are our only true belongings?" What do I want my "true belongings" to be?

15

SEEKING THE TRUE SELF

On Facing Our Faults

If someone commits a fault while at any work—while working in the kitchen, in the storeroom, in serving in the bakery, in the garden, in any craft or anywhere else—she or he must at once come before the prioress or abbot and community and admit this fault and make satisfaction.

—FROM CHAPTER 46, "FAULTS COMMITTED IN OTHER MATTERS"

Kerry Egan is a hospice chaplain who lives in Columbia, South Carolina. She has served as a companion to countless people in the final weeks of their lives. I met her when we both spoke at a conference of the American Benedictine Academy, a group of vowed and lay people who work to impart Benedictine values in today's world. According to Kerry, what makes the transition harder for so many people facing death is not fear of the unknown, or even the physical decline that accompanies end of life. It is the secrets and regrets we harbor from the past.

In her book *On Living,* Kerry tells the story of one of her favorite patients, a woman she calls Gloria. Gloria had become pregnant when she was nineteen. Like many young women of her time, she had few choices. She felt pressured to give up her child for adoption. She did not want to do this. After she turned the child over to an adoption agency, Gloria woke in the middle of the night with the aching need to take back her son. The woman who handled the adoption assured her she would only be harming the child. How could she, a single teenager, earning a modest secretary's salary, properly care for a baby? Gloria was told her son would be much better off being raised by a married couple with financial means. Gloria's parents agreed. They chose not to help their daughter.

Gloria was undeterred. She returned again to the adoption agency. She was told she would have to reimburse the agency for the month's care it had given her and the child. Gloria effectively would have to buy back her son. Still, she pressed on. She sold her books. She sold her jewelry. She sold all of her clothing, except one outfit and pair of shoes for work. She even sold her hair curlers. Finally, the agency turned over her child. Her grandmother agreed to allow Gloria and the baby to live with her. Eventually, Gloria married, and her husband raised her son as his own. There was one problem, though. Gloria never told her son what had transpired. She kept the truth buried inside her. Now, in her final weeks, the true story was banging at the chambers of her heart, begging to come out.

Gloria asked Kerry if she would tell her son the truth on her behalf. They talked about this and then discussed it some more. She then asked Kerry to at least be in the room with her when she told her son. One day, Gloria informed Kerry she had gone ahead on her own and revealed her secret.

"You're the only thing that matters to me now," Gloria's son told her, "and I love you."

Perhaps you could have seen this ending coming. But Gloria could not envision that ending for herself. For decades, she had carried her secret like a satchel of ballast.

The early monastics were keen observers of their own behavior. They spent considerable time in solitude, but they also lived in the teeming cauldron of community. They understood that human beings can and will screw up—even those who seek holiness with a single-minded purpose. They didn't deny this. They didn't try to repress their urges, or flee from them. Instead, they said: speak these failings aloud. Hold them to the light and you will rob them of their power over you.

St. Benedict exhorts his community members to admit faults as soon as they happen. But admit them, he says, only to those who can be trusted, to those who *know how to heal their own wounds*. We don't need to confess them on *Ellen* or *Inside Edition*, or write a letter to the editor, or shout our mistakes from the rooftop. Those to whom we reveal our faults are to safeguard our trust. Our secrets aren't material for office gossip or the family grapevine. We cradle with reverence what is shared, as Kerry Egan, the hospice nurse did, when entrusted with the hidden truth about Gloria's son.

> *When the cause of sin lies hidden in the conscience, [one]*
> *is to reveal it only to the prioress or abbot, or to one of*
> *the spiritual elders who know how to heal their own*
> *wounds as well as those of others without exposing them*
> *and making them public.*

—FROM CHAPTER 46, "FAULTS
COMMITTED IN OTHER MATTERS"

Confronting faults is step one on the path to finding the true self. I am one of those people who goes around trying to camouflage a host of insecurities with various emotional face powders. I must be pretty good at it. People often comment after they get to know me that they found me intimidating at first. This is laughable to me, since I am a breathing, walking pack of anxieties. I may not want people I barely know peering into my satchel of vulnerabilities, but I don't want to be off-putting either. I often feel like St. Paul: I do the things I don't want to do and don't do the things I know I should. Mostly, I want to be seen for the complex person I am—someone who, yes, is prone to piques of anger and bouts of insecurity, but is also compassionate, loyal, and trustworthy.

In those times when I do make myself vulnerable—when I admit that I often feel I'm not a good enough writer, a good enough journalist, a good enough wife or stepmother—I'm often amazed at what happens. Others reveal to me parts of myself I'd lost track of. They remind me of who I am, in all my complexity. Likewise, when I show my true self—or at least my *truer* self—I give others permission to be who they are too, without fear of rejection.

In reporting a radio segment on a cancer center chaplain, I had the chance to interview a young mother—a mental health specialist who had been diagnosed with advanced breast cancer.

She described the experience of living with cancer as suffering "a layer of losses." She had lost her health, her stamina, her hair, not to mention a part of her body that identified her as a woman. She had lost a future she once imagined for herself. She wondered who she now was.

"I'm alive, but what is my identity?" she asked. "How do I find meaning in my life now without being the person I was before?"

At the same time, those losses forced her to shed many of the labels she had used to measure herself as a person. They led her, ultimately, to a truer sense of self. "The truth is," she said, "we are all loveable and worthy without all the markers we fall back on every day to make ourselves feel worthwhile." Cancer, she told me, had set her free "to love myself without those identifiers. And that allows me to feel love for everyone else."

In college, one of the most memorable courses I took was called "Graham Greene: A Novelist Looks At Religion." In Greene's novels, characters that are the most troubled turn out to be the most compassionate. In *The Power and the Glory*, the "whiskey priest" breaks his vows by fathering a child. Even so, at a time in Mexico when the church and the clergy are being repressed, he risks his life to bring the Eucharist to others. In *The End of the Affair,* an unfaithful wife who identifies with the pain of another brings about a small miracle. In *The Heart of the Matter*, it is a policeman tortured by his own sins and convinced of his own impending condemnation who ends up showing the most genuine faith.

As I age, I realize that I don't so much desire to be seen as flawless, but rather as both flawed *and* still worthy. Worthy of receiving love and of giving love. From the monastic elders, I've learned that I am not my faults any more than I am my thoughts or my emotions. My thoughts and emotions need not control me. It is only when I force them into the substratum of my heart that they gain the power to overwhelm me. A psychologist I know often says he doesn't have to like every one of his patients. There are some he finds mean-spirited, self-absorbed, or shallow. How then does he manage to treat them? "I keep myself aware of my feelings," he says. "I don't confuse my feelings of dislike with the patient sitting in front of me."

I occasionally attend workshops given by the Centering Prayer group where I live. In one of those workshops, we learned the Welcoming Prayer. When we pray the Welcoming Prayer, we acknowledge what is troubling us—I am angry I did not get the assignment I wanted. . . . I am frustrated that I have to work so hard. . . . I resent being the person who gets stuck with the cleaning up. . . . All of these issues have to do with some wound to our sense of self. In the Welcoming Prayer, we acknowledge what we are experiencing, and welcome it in:

> *I let go of my desire for security, for survival. Welcome.*
> *I let go of my desire for approval and affection. Welcome.*
> *I let go of my desire for power and control. Welcome.*
> *I let go of my desire to change (any person, situation,*
> *event, feeling, emotion). Welcome.*

It is a way of passing through the experience, rather than obsessing about it, running away from it, or trying to stuff it into the unconscious—where it will fester, but never disappear.

In one of his most famous poems, the Sufi poet Rumi compares the human heart to a guest house. Every morning, he says, there is a new arrival, including the often unexpected and unwelcome visits of depression, meanness, envy, shame, malice, and myriad dark thoughts. Welcome each guest in, the poet says, and treat each one honorably. *Be grateful for whoever comes / because each has been sent / as a guide from beyond.*

I have come to see my flaws and my faults as guests—unwelcome ones, to be sure, but part of my life nonetheless. How do I transform them from adversaries into *guides from beyond,* as Rumi puts it? I invite them in, and welcome them to sit with me at the table for a while. Have a cup of tea, I say. Let's talk before I send you on your way. Maybe we can learn to become friends.

For Reflection:

~ What are the faults I most struggle with? Is there a way for me to befriend these faults and remove some of their power over me?

~ What secrets do I harbor? Can I visualize revealing those to someone I trust, or to a person who needs to know the truth? What does that feel like?

~ Was there a time when a family member, friend, or mentor helped reveal to me parts of myself I had forgotten? What was that experience like?

~ How well have I shown reverence for the secrets and faults others have revealed to me?

~ What characters in literature, film, or theater have helped me understand how to be both good *and* flawed?

16

SUMMONING THE COMMUNITY FOR COUNSEL

On Building Consensus

The prioress or abbot shall call the whole community together and explain what the business is; and after hearing the advice of the members, ponder it and follow what she or he judges the wiser course.

—FROM CHAPTER 3, "SUMMONING
THE COMMUNITY FOR COUNSEL"

In one of the radio stations where I've worked, a new station manager called a meeting to explain his goals to the staff. In the course of the meeting, he announced he was canceling a regular poetry feature the station had been airing for years. Granted, our poetry program didn't have the following of say, the weekend folk music show or our current affairs shows, but as a pubic station, we're responsible for providing a range of programming reflecting the variety of our listeners' interests.

When I challenged our new manager to reconsider the move, he said his decision was final. When I asked why the show couldn't continue in perhaps some revised form, he answered, "Because I said so."

There was stunned silence in the room. It wasn't because I had dared to challenge the new boss, or even because of his answer, one that sounded more like an exasperated parent addressing a child, not a manager responding to a colleague. What troubled the staff was that our manager hadn't bothered to consult us, to sound out our opinions before making a decision.

The story has a happy ending. This particular manager is basically a good guy. He quickly sensed how poorly that episode unfolded. After that, he shared information more readily. He kept the staff apprised of major changes in the offing, so we could at least have a chance to offer input. Over time, he's became much more of a Benedictine manager.

When I worked for the *Wall Street Journal,* most of the companies I reported on professed to value their workers' involvement. "Participatory management" is the term they used. Few corporations, however, actually practice it, preferring a top-down model of management. One of my earliest beats was covering the airline industry. This was during a period of frequent mergers and acquisitions. Inevitably, airlines would describe the transaction as a merger of equals. But the acquiring company usually came out on top. Their employees would end up with more seniority and better benefits, at least at the outset.

It may simply be wired into our DNA to fight to protect our turf, or to want to prevail. After a series of air accidents in the 1980s and early 1990s, several airlines began training their pilots in "cockpit resource management." It was an attempt to improve communication, coordination, and cooperation on the flight deck. In one of the more dramatic accidents, involving an Air Florida flight out of Washington DC in 1982, the captain ignored warnings from the first officer that ice had accumulated on the aircraft's wings, compromising its lift. On takeoff, the plane plummeted into an iced-over Potomac River, killing nearly everyone on board. In 1985, Delta Airlines Flight 191 crashed while landing in a thunderstorm outside Dallas-Fort Worth.

"Lightning coming out of that one," the first officer had warned the captain before the aircraft entered a dark cumulonimbus cloud buildup.

"Where?" is all that the captain replied.

The first officer continued on with the landing. The plane entered the buildup and encountered a violent downdraft a few hundred feet from the ground. It crashed just short of the runway.

I was allowed as a reporter to attend a cockpit resource management training one of the airlines was holding in New York. I was assigned to be part of a three-person flight deck crew. We were given a scenario in which we had to make a decision about whether to continue a landing, or abort. The captain thought we should forge on, the first officer didn't. I, taking the part of a second officer, said we should choose the most cautious course. But the pilot who favored landing kept insisting he was right. Finally, he wore me down to the point where I didn't want to argue about this any longer. The other pilot seemed willing to give his captain the benefit of the doubt. We pressed on with the landing. After the exercise, we learned that our decision would have doomed everyone on board. Even though we were all merely playing roles, I still regret having given in to the one pilot's bullying and not standing my ground for what I believed to be safe.

We do the best we can when we have decisions to make. Luckily, the kind of split-second decisions that confronted those pilots are not the kind of decisions that most companies, or families, routinely face. We can learn from how monasteries arrive at decisions. Monastic decision-making is a slow, deliberate process of discernment. Its goal is consensus.

First, the books are opened, so to speak. Everyone receives the same amount of information and data. (In most corporate settings, only the board of trustees, the lawyers, and top management would have access to detailed financial information). Every community member gets an equal chance to weigh in, regardless of age, seniority, or position. Here again, St. Benedict upended the customs of his time, in which only men of a certain class were afforded decision-making authority. He showed a healthy respect for the fresh ideas that might emanate from the youngest in age.

> *The reason why we have said all should be called to counsel is that the Spirit often reveals what is better to the younger.*
>
> —FROM CHAPTER 3, "SUMMONING THE COMMUNITY FOR COUNSEL"

We've all probably attended public meetings where people talk over one another, or engage in booing, applauding, and all manner of unruly behavior. St. Benedict wants none of that. At monastic meetings, there are to be no overt displays of either support or dissent.

> *The community members, for their part, are to express*
> *their opinions with all humility, and not to presume to*
> *defend their own views obstinately.*
>
> —FROM CHAPTER 3, "SUMMONING
> THE COMMUNITY FOR COUNSEL"

A good example of decision-making by consensus is the way the sisters of Mount St. Benedict Monastery in Erie, Pennsylvania, deliberated over whether to close their academy for girls. St. Benedict's Academy had been a fixture for more than a century in Erie's inner city. But by the late 1980s, many of the middle-class Catholic families had moved out of the city center to other neighborhoods or the suburbs. Enrollment dropped from a high of six hundred to about one hundred and fifty students. Erie had three Catholic secondary schools, two of them for girls only. Most of the Academy's students needed tuition assistance. The sisters had to decide whether to continue making the academy the focus of their fundraising efforts, or redirect their work and financial resources to other ministries aimed at helping the poor.

"It was a very emotional thing, not a decision we could make on pure logic," recalls Sister Mary Ellen Plumb, who taught at the academy. Eight of the community's sisters were on staff at the school, and a large number of them were themselves Academy graduates.

The first thing the sisters did was to bring in an outside facilitator, "somebody not emotionally involved," Sister Mary Ellen says.

Each community member received a fact sheet along with financial data. For months before the final meetings took place, the sisters prayed for discernment. As the decision drew closer, they spent an entire day "wrapped in prayer," as Sister Mary Ellen puts it.

Each sister who wanted to express an opinion had a chance to speak for or against keeping the school. There were table discussions in small groups. It soon became clear which way the majority was leaning. Because it was such a big decision, each sister was asked to individually state her position. Finally, Sister Mary Ellen gave her own tearful consent.

"In the end, we agreed there was not as much need for the academy as there was for other ministries for the poor," she recalls.

Once a decision is made in a monastic setting, the whole community agrees to pull in the same direction. Even those who oppose it agree to try to make it work; no throwing stones from the outside in.

Ritual plays a large part in bringing community members to a place of acceptance. This is something few enterprises consider as a way of bringing closure when a company moves out of town, reduces its workforce significantly, or shuts down all together. On the night the Erie sisters publicly announced they had agreed to close the school, community members gathered in the chapel. They surrounded the eight sisters who were on the school's faculty and prayed for them. "That was an incredible moment," Sister Mary Ellen says. The prayer service ended with each member of the community sharing a kiss of peace. "Everyone was very gracious to those who had (originally) voted differently from the majority."

The amount of time and prayer that goes into monastic decision-making would not likely take place in a business setting. But the transparency, the openness with which decisions are made, and the willingness to listen to all points of view can serve as a model for both decision-making and consensus-building in business—as well as in our families.

Good to their word, the Erie sisters threw their energy and resources into new ministries. Freed from the financial drain of the school, they expanded the services of their local soup kitchen and opened a neighborhood arts center where at-risk youth learn to paint, play musical instruments, write poetry, and make crafts. Only two months after their beloved academy closed, it was transformed into a bustling education center that offers English as a Second Language, GED classes, and job readiness programs for Erie's poor and its growing immigrant communities.

Sister Mary Ellen says the chapter on humility in *The Rule* is a good preparation for entering into any deliberation. It reminds us that no one person possesses all the truth, or is right one hundred percent of the time. All of us hold within us a piece of the wisdom needed to move forward. Often, the best path of progress is the winding way of consensus.

For Reflection:

:~ How are decisions made in my workplace and my home? Am I sometimes bullied into going along with a decision, as in the cockpit management training session? How have I reacted? How would I like to react?

:~ How can the monastic practices that lead to consensus apply to decisions I need to make?

:~ How do I react when my view is the minority view, and I must accept the decision of the majority?

:~ Are there ways I can peacefully, and with humility, accept being on the losing side of an issue?

:~ How does the chapter in *The Rule* on humility serve as a guide for decision-making by consensus?

17

THE CARE OF SOULS

To Be a Leader

Excitable, anxious, extreme, obstinate, jealous or over-suspicious she or he must not be. Such a [leader] is never at rest.

—FROM CHAPTER 64, "ELECTION OF A PRIORESS OR ABBOT"

I'm an avid tea drinker, but have many friends who are coffee fanatics. They suffer withdrawal if they can't find a Starbucks nearby. They'll gladly fork over nearly three times as much for a Starbucks "tall" as they would for a similar size cup of coffee at McDonald's or Denny's. This love affair is fueled partly by atmosphere—the sense that when you step inside a Starbucks, you enter what the company describes as "that third place between home and work." There, in a den-like décor, you can sit undisturbed for hours, sipping coffee customized to taste. Frappucino or macchiato? Soy milk or skim? Raw sugar or honey?

Howard Schultz is the man largely responsible for Starbucks' distinctive allure. Fellow CEOs admire him for building a $29 billion enterprise that spans thirty-seven countries. To me, that is the least of his accomplishments. Schultz grew up in public housing, sold his blood to help pay his college tuition, and was the first in his immediate family to earn a degree. He worked his way up from an entry-level job to corporate chieftain. Today, Starbucks offers health benefits to all of its employees and reimburses workers who complete college degrees through online courses.

Asked to name the leaders he most admires, Schultz doesn't mention other CEOs, political figures, or even famous philanthropists. He cites a rabbi and a pope.

"Nothing I've heard or read in the past few years," Schultz wrote in the *New York Times,* "has rivaled the power of the image I viewed on my cellphone a few years ago: Pope Francis shortly after his election, kneeling and washing the feet of a dozen prisoners in Rome, one of them a young Muslim woman."

Schultz also wrote of visiting Jerusalem's Western Wall, a holy site where visitors leave small scraps of paper between the cracks containing their written prayers. He traveled there with a well-known spiritual leader, the Israeli rabbi Nosson Tzvi Finkel. As the two approached, Schultz noticed Finkel pause about ten feet from the wall. He beckoned to his friend to come nearer. "I've never been closer than this," the rabbi said. "You go, I am not worthy."

It takes extreme confidence, not to mention courage, to shepherd a company, a not-for-profit organization, a government agency, a synagogue, or a church. But how many leaders have a strong enough sense of self to acknowledge publicly, "I am not worthy?"

In interviews, Shultz talks often of "leading from the heart." But what does it mean to lead that way? Is it possible to both succeed and be compassionate? Is it a path only for the rare executive like Schultz? Or is there a way to balance profitability and practical management with spiritual pursuits?

These are questions St. Benedict wrestled with in the 6th century. He places his thoughts on leadership at the very start of *The Rule*. I don't believe he gives this topic a prominent place because he exalts the leader of a monastery above others. To the contrary, he warns monastic leaders not to become *puffed up* or place their personal interests above those of others. *Only in this are we distinguished*, he writes, *if we are found better than others in good works and humility*. Good works and humility. Hardly topics found in MBA programs or professional development seminars.

Benedict's vision of a leader isn't the hard-charging, admit–no-mistakes, type A personalities whose faces often adorn the covers of *Fortune* and *Forbes*. In Benedict's management manual, *servant* is another name for leader. Servant leaders don't acquire companies in order to dismantle them. They don't accept bonuses after laying off workers, cutting their wages, or causing the company's stock to collapse. They don't lunch on an expense account or fly across the country in a private jet while slashing per diems for lower-rung employees who travel coach. They don't take salaries that are three hundred times what their workers are paid.

In a Benedictine world view, the best leaders are teachers, not dictators. Perhaps the most revolutionary of all Benedict's ideas on leadership is the model he asks us to imitate: Christ.

> *The prioress or abbot must always remember what she or he is . . . aware that more will be expected of one to whom more has been entrusted . . . Anyone who receives the name of prioress or abbot is to lead disciples . . . by living example.*
>
> —FROM CHAPTER 2, "QUALITIES OF THE PRIORESS OR ABBOT"

But Benedict is also a realist. He recognizes not every employee is going to start out a hard worker, eager learner, or good listener. Some will be *stubborn and dull*. The best leaders draw out good qualities in others by modeling those qualities themselves. He also understood monasteries have to work smart. They should be self-supporting. They shouldn't take on too much debt. They should aim to generate enough revenue to cover costs and store up reserves for emergencies and lean times. While these practical affairs have their place, Benedict also reminds us that leaders mustn't become so obsessed with results that they neglect the well-being of those they supervise. Whether one works in the business world, in education, politics, the not-for-profit sector, or as head of a monastery, a leader's foremost concern is people. Or, as Benedict puts it so beautifully, *the care of souls*.

> *Above all, [the monastery's leaders] must not show too great concern for the fleeting and temporal things of this world, neglecting or treating lightly the welfare of those entrusted to them. Rather they should keep in mind that they have undertaken the care of souls for whom they must give account.*
>
> —FROM CHAPTER 2, "QUALITIES OF THE PRIORESS OR ABBOT"

Throughout my career in journalism, I've been privileged to work for managers who put people first and understand *the care of souls*. They listen with the ear of the heart in order to lead from the heart.

Reporters for the *Wall Street Journal* cover the news from a network of national and international bureaus. When I joined the paper, I went to work in the Chicago bureau. The bureau chief there was Sue Shellenbarger, a person who came to define for me what it means to be a servant leader who cares for souls.

Before becoming a supervisor, Sue had distinguished herself as an agriculture reporter. Because she had done the same kind of work as the reporters she was now managing, she understood well the demands they faced. Benedictine writer Joan Chittister once described the qualities essential to the prioress or abbot of a monastery. "They are not about giving orders, but calling out the best in others," she wrote. "They are not about cultivating slaves, underlings or servants. [Their] way of leadership is about relationship." Sue Shellenbarger epitomized those qualities.

Sue had a practice of taking her reporters out individually every few months for breakfast or lunch. It was her way of "checking in" with each of us outside the confines of the office and the routine discussions we shared on a daily basis. I particularly remember a breakfast meeting we had during my first year on the job.

Sue started out by saying she had no complaints with my work. I was working hard and had broken news many times on my beat. She noticed, however, that I seemed preoccupied. She asked if everything was all right. I told her, actually, it wasn't. I'd recently learned that a friend of mine was suffering from AIDS. In fact, he was dying. Some mutual friends were making arrangements to take him into their home to care for him.

"Have you ever thought about seeing a counselor?" Sue asked.

"No, why?" I said. "Do you think I need a therapist?"

"I do," she answered. "Do you know why?"

"Sure. You want me to succeed at the *Wall Street Journal.*"

"No, Judy. It's because I want you to succeed at your life."

I want you to succeed at your life. I'll never forget those words. The best managers know it isn't about them. It's about *us*. It's about searching for the key that unleashes the potential inside an employee that may lie untapped.

> *Prioresses or abbots must know that anyone undertaking the charge of souls must be ready to account for them . . . Let them realize that on judgment day, they will surely have to submit a reckoning to God for all their souls— and indeed for their own as well . . . If they teach disciples that something is not to be done, then neither should they do it.*
>
> —FROM CHAPTER 2, "QUALITIES OF THE PRIORESS OR ABBOT"

I've also experienced the opposite end of the spectrum. For nearly two years, I worked as a reporter in London. By the time I was assigned there, I'd won numerous writing awards and twice been a finalist for the Pulitzer Prize in journalism. My editor quickly made it clear he didn't want me reporting the kinds of human interest feature stories I loved to write and felt I did best. Instead, he wanted me to focus on business reporting—the kinds of stories *he* thought I should write.

He would often hand back my copy marked in red ink, the way a high school teacher might correct a student's composition. He monitored the time I arrived at the office in the morning and when I left for home. Once, when I spoke up in defense of some work I had done, he threatened to walk out of the room if I continued. He compared me unfavorably to other reporters he supervised. They were the go-along, get-along types who didn't question his decisions. You can probably guess that I didn't fall into that category. I often felt his public praise for others was a thinly veiled way of trying to further erode my confidence.

> *Prioresses and abbots should avoid all favoritism in the*
> *monastery. They are not to love one more than another*
> *unless they find someone better in good works.*
> —FROM CHAPTER 2, "QUALITIES OF THE PRIORESS OR ABBOT"

The comparisons with other reporters, the red-lining of my copy, and other criticisms—far from improving my work—only led to a more precipitous decline. I felt so off balance, I began to wonder if whatever writing talent I once possessed had simply disappeared in crossing the Atlantic.

St. Benedict, far ahead of his time, recognized that human beings are complex creatures. We don't all respond to the same prompts. A good leader, he says, will *accommodate and adapt himself to each one's character and intelligence.* Notice, he doesn't say the flock—in other words, the employees—must contort themselves to adapt to a manager's personality. Quite the opposite. It is the manager's responsibility to draw out the best from those entrusted to his or her care.

> *[They] must know what a difficult and demanding bur-*
> *den they have undertaken: directing souls and serving a*
> *variety of temperaments, coaxing, reproving and encourag-*
> *ing them as appropriate. They must so accommodate and*
> *adapt themselves to each one's character and intelligence*
> *that they will not only keep the flock entrusted to their care*
> *from dwindling, but will rejoice in a good flock.*
> —FROM CHAPTER 2, "QUALITIES OF THE PRIORESS OR ABBOT"

As I arrived for work as usual one crisp autumn morning, my editor called me into his office. I knew something serious was coming when he closed the door behind him.

"I have very bad news for you," he said curtly. "You're being laid off."

My first reaction was, "This has got to be a joke. I've just been a finalist for the Pulitzer Prize." Then he began rattling off from a piece of paper in front of him, "Your termination date is . . . Your severance package is . . . " I remember thinking that it had taken me fifteen years to that point to build my career and fifteen seconds for all that I'd worked for to come crashing down.

In the US, we call this being "let go." But the English have a more apt expression. They call it being "made redundant." It is as if you are being told your model is outdated, no longer necessary or desirable. So much of my identity hinged on being a reporter. The layoff felt like a sucker punch to my sense of self-worth.

I was not the only staff person let go that day. None of us were given a specific reason, other than the layoff was for "economic reasons." Still, I couldn't help but think the stormy relationship with my supervisor didn't aid my cause when my employer went scouting for people to cut.

Looking back on the experience with greater understanding, I can empathize to some degree with my editor. He probably thought I was undisciplined and obstinate—more trouble than I was worth. St. Benedict doesn't sugarcoat the burdens of leadership. The shepherd will encounter a *disobedient flock,* he warns. *The Rule* even says the abbot would be justified in giving the worst offenders what we might describe as a swift kick in the butt—a reaction perhaps common in the 6th century, but hardly appropriate today! Yet, the idea holds. Being too softhearted or wishy-washy doesn't work, but neither does being consistently harsh. The best leaders will *vary with circumstances.*

The prioress or abbot should always observe the Apostle's recommendation, in which is said: "Use argument, appeal, reproof" (2 Tim 4:2). This means that they must vary with circumstances, threatening and coaxing by turns, stern as a taskmaster, devoted and tender as only a parent can be.

—FROM CHAPTER 2, "QUALITIES OF THE PRIORESS OR ABBOT"

In my work experience, it was my Chicago bureau chief who was *tender and devoted* as a parent—and as tough as one—when she needed to be. She took care to listen for what I hadn't expressed verbally. She noticed my sadness when my friend was dying—and was attuned enough to ask about it. But she also paid attention when I slacked in my duties. I once arrived late for work on a day I was to oversee the bureau's spot news desk—an important source of breaking news for our business readers. Sue bluntly told me to never let that happen again. Still, I never sensed that she defined the totality of my work by a single misstep, or even a few. She corrected me in a way that let me know that she knew I was capable of doing better. When someone does this, it's not a personal attack. It's an appeal, and in some ways even a vote of confidence that we will learn from our mistake.

As it turned out, what appeared to be a heartbreaking setback developed into one of the biggest opportunities of my career. I left daily journalism for a while to pursue other kinds of writing I had wanted to do, but hadn't the time. I now look upon the day I was let go as a kind of second birthday.

Management expert Christine Porath has studied extensively the relationships between supervisors and their employees. Managers who are rude and belittle end up with workers who don't perform as well as those whose bosses treat them with respect.

"Incivility shuts people down in other ways too," Porath says. "Employees contribute less and lose their conviction." Like St. Benedict, Porath emphasizes a listening heart. "Listening, smiling, sharing, and thanking others . . . can have a huge impact."

> *When the prioress or abbot must punish them, they should*
> *use prudence and avoid extremes; otherwise, by rubbing*
> *too hard to remove the rust, they may break the vessel.*
> —FROM CHAPTER 64, "THE ELECTION OF A PRIORESS OR ABBOT"

One of the most memorable business stories I covered involved the demise of the Houston-based energy company Enron Corp. It also taught me some important lessons about how *not* to be a leader. Enron's executives engaged in a series of accounting gimmicks that made it appear the corporation's subsidiaries were generating substantial profits for the parent company. Essentially the same pot of money kept circulating around each of the subsidiaries; it was one big Ponzi scheme.

Enron's corporate culture fed this kind of gamesmanship. The company created monopolies to drive up energy prices in markets it served, particularly on the West Coast. When its customers struggled to pay Enron's inflated prices, executives callously joked at staff meetings, "Let the last person in L.A. turn out the lights."

Many of Enron's top managers, people once dubbed by analysts as "the smartest guys in the room," were later indicted and eventually went to jail. Within their communities, they had been pillars of their churches, leaders in the synagogue. What produced this Sunday to Monday disconnect? Why would otherwise religious, law-abiding citizens break the law at work? And why didn't Enron's rank and file employees—themselves company stockholders—question their managers' actions? Did the intense drive to succeed subsume everything else?

Unbridled ambition also propelled a scandal involving one of the world's most successful automakers. In his drive to make Volkswagen the world's number one automaker, CEO Martin Winterkorn pushed for increased sales of diesel-fuel models. There was a big problem, though. To boost sales in the US, Volkswagen's diesel cars needed to meet emissions standards for nitrogen oxides that were tougher than Europe's regulations. The company decided to cheat. It rigged its cars with software that made it seem as though they were emitting fewer pollutants than the law allowed. This is no abstract example of a victimless crime. Nitrogen oxides have been linked to a host of respiratory and cardiovascular illnesses. They worsen the suffering of people with asthma and pulmonary disease, especially in the elderly.

The Volkswagen scandal followed another high profile case, in which General Motors failed to correct faulty ignition switches in several of its models. The flaw caused engines to shut down while the car was in motion, resulting in more than a hundred and fifty deaths. GM had known about the defect for decades, but failed to fix it.

St. Benedict offers a prescription for leaders seeking to avoid the moral quagmires that ruined Enron and sullied the public's trust in Volkswagen and GM. *Speak the truth with heart and tongue.* And, perhaps more pointedly, *Day by day, remind yourself you are going to die. Hour by hour, keep careful watch over all you do, aware that God's gaze is upon you wherever you may be.*

Analyses of what went wrong at Enron didn't expose a company full of evil people. It was in fact a company of ordinary people, heir to the kinds of preoccupations that to some extent plague all of us who want to succeed. What motivated the managers of

Enron, and quite possibly Volkswagen and GM, to do what they did? The most common of impulses. Fear of losing the wealth to which they'd grown accustomed. Fear of admitting failure. Fear of looking weak in the press and among peers. Fear of losing their status as "the smartest guys in the room."

To counteract these very human tendencies, St. Benedict reminds us that more is expected of those to whom much has been entrusted. *Remember what is written,* he says: *Seek first the kingdom of God and his justice, and all these things will be given you as well.* And again, *Those who fear him lack nothing.*

The Rule gives us another important leadership model in the person known as the monastic "cellarer." The title rarely is used in monasteries today, but the cellarer's duties remain. Cellarers are similar to office managers. They oversee inventory, making sure people have what they need to do their work. Traditionally, the cellarer handed out food and was responsible for meeting the material needs of community members. It could be a heady job, having control over goods and deciding who gets what. It's perhaps no surprise that St. Benedict devotes an entire chapter to the cellarer's qualifications, and carefully outlines the type of person he or she must be.

> Someone who is wise, mature in conduct, temperate, not
> an excessive eater, not proud, excitable, offensive, dilatory
> or wasteful, but God-fearing, like a parent to the whole
> community.
>
> —FROM CHAPTER 31, "QUALIFICATIONS OF
> THE MONASTERY CELLARER"

Office managers are often among the most harried people in a business. Who would blame them for growing annoyed at times with continuous demands? *The Rule* asks more of these leaders. If someone comes with an unrealistic demand, it's not to be met with a snarky, sarcastic remark, but understanding and compassion.

> *If any member happens to make an unreasonable demand, [the cellarer] should not reject her or him with disdain and cause distress, but reasonably and humbly deny the improper request.*
>
> —FROM CHAPTER 31, "QUALIFICATIONS OF THE MONASTERY CELLARER"

In other words, if you have to turn someone down, do it gently. I once served as head of a search committee for a Catholic publisher seeking to hire a new CEO. Let me tell you, it was a dreadful task to have to call the also-rans—many of whom were highly qualified people—and tell them they didn't get the job. Taking a cue from the chapter on the cellarer, I tried to emphasize what each person had to offer, that it was a close decision, and that any company would be fortunate to have them on board, even though it didn't work out for them with this particular position.

> *Above all, be humble. If goods are not available to meet a request, [the cellarer] will offer a kind word in reply, for it is written: "A kind word is better than the best gift." (Sir 18:17)*
>
> —FROM CHAPTER 31, "QUALIFICATIONS OF THE MONASTERY CELLARER"

The expression of kindness is a particularly Benedictine mandate. It represents the best way of guarding against what Benedict sees as a particularly insidious threat to the smooth and peaceful operation of any enterprise: *grumbling.* The kind of gossiping, complaining, and bad-mouthing that can turn a workplace, and even a home, into a toxic dump. *We absolutely condemn in all places vulgarity and gossip,* Benedict says in the chapter on "Restraint of Speech." And, elsewhere, *First and foremost, there must be no word or sign of the evil of grumbling, no manifestation of it for any reason at all.*

It's clear whom he considers responsible for provoking the kind of justifiable grumbling that prevents members of any community—be it monastic, business, government, or otherwise—from serving one another in love. It is the community's leaders. Those who become overwhelmed by their responsibilities should seek additional help, he says, so kindness doesn't become a casualty. Let no one be distressed or disquieted.

The chapter on the cellarer reminds us too that a Benedictine vision of leadership isn't confined only to the top brass, the men in white collars and women in power suits. As a teenager, I worked after school at a clothing store in my hometown of Bayonne, New Jersey. The stockroom where new shipments arrived was the dustiest, dingiest part of the store. Working there involved largely mindless tasks, like unpacking merchandise and pinning price tags onto the plastic covers of blouses and pajamas. Yet high school girls like me, hired primarily for the sales floor, would jump at the chance to work in the stockroom. It was because of Angie and Josie, the two little Italian ladies who ran that part of the store.

Every day, Angie and Josie placed a fresh plate of cookies on the break room table for their employees. They stocked the kitchenette with teas and hot chocolate. They treated shipments of skirts, slacks, and ladies lingerie as if they were buried treasure. In that sense, they were like monastic cellarers who are urged to *regard all utensils and goods of the monastery as sacred vessels. Nothing is to be neglected.* That was Angie and Josie's approach to their work.

These two women pass my servant leadership test in other ways, too. They were congenial managers, genuinely interested in the lives of the silly high school girls who worked for them. Whether it was a romantic crush gone wrong, a conflict with one of our parents, or our struggles to fit in with the popular girls at school, none of our adolescent woes were too piddling a subject for their listening hearts. *Nothing is to be neglected.*

> *Let them strive to be loved rather than feared.*
> —FROM CHAPTER 64, "THE ELECTION
> OF A PRIORESS OR ABBOT"

Angie and Josie would probably laugh heartily at my characterizing them as leaders. They thought of themselves as a couple of hardworking women in smocks and sensible shoes. Long before I learned the importance in monastic life of showing hospitality to strangers, I saw it at work in Angie and Josie. They treated all who worked for them with a hospitality of heart. Like my bureau chief in Chicago, like the abbot, prioress, and cellarer described in *The Rule,* Angie and Josie remain for me not only examples of servant leadership, but of true success.

For Reflection:

∾ How would I describe the leaders I admire and the qualities they have I would like to emulate? Are any like Angie and Josie, who don't fit the conventional definition of a manager?

∾ What would I include in a list of "habits of the heart" that could make me a more compassionate and effective leader? Here are some examples:

  ¤ Choose imagination over image

  ¤ Listen to others: it is how I will learn

  ¤ Compensation isn't everything, but balance is

  ¤ Be the first to respect others

  ¤ We can all be winners

∾ How do the lines in *The Rule—Day by day, remind yourself you are going to die. Hour by hour, keep careful watch over all you do*—relate to becoming a better leader?

∾ Was there a time at work when I "listened with the ear of the heart" to another person who didn't verbally express any difficulty, as Sue Shellenbarger did? What was that experience like?

∾ Do I tend to be hard on those I supervise? What might be behind that? Is there a way to supervise differently?

18

NOTHING IS TO
BE NEGLECTED

On Caring for What We Have

Regard all utensils and goods of the monastery as sacred
vessels of the altar, aware that nothing is to be neglected.

—FROM CHAPTER 31, "QUALIFICATIONS
OF THE MONASTERY CELLARER"

Whenever I step inside a monastery, I'm always impressed with the physical beauty of the surroundings. From the chapel artwork and woodcraft to the flower gardens and the often handmade centerpieces on the dining room tables, nothing escapes care. Rarely can you spot so much as a mite of dust in a corner. Unlike my dining room table and work desk at home, there is a distinct lack of clutter. Every item rests in its place.

In his 2015 encyclical *Laudate Si*, Pope Francis called care of the environment a Christian value. More than fifteen hundred years ago, monasteries recognized that *nothing is to be neglected*. That hasn't been true in most cultures. In central Illinois, where I live, the Illinois River is a powerful presence. It cuts through some of the richest glacial soil for growing crops in all of North America. A natural resources specialist I interviewed told me that at one time, we pumped so much effluent into the river that even the water in household toilet bowls was more sanitary.

Happily, that is no longer the case, thanks to advances in wastewater treatment. But would the river have become polluted, our topsoil degraded with toxins, and our breathing air contaminated with hazardous gases, if from the start we had treated these critical natural resources as *vessels of the altar?*

In his book *Always We Begin Again: The Benedictine Way of Living,* attorney John McQuiston writes, "Everything we have is on loan. Our homes, businesses, rivers, closest relationships, bodies and experiences. Everything we have is ours in trust and must be returned at the end of our use of it." Increasingly, Americans are recognizing (as monastics did so many centuries ago) that there is a limit to what we can take from nature.

Several astronauts who traveled to the moon were asked in a documentary to describe their experiences in space. Nearly all of them spoke of how precarious the earth appeared, suspended like a small bead in a vast cobalt sea. Piers J. Sellers, who made three shuttle flights to the International Space Station, said of his journeys, "I watched hurricanes cartwheel across the oceans, the Amazon snake its way to the sea through a brilliant green carpet of forest, and gigantic nighttime thunderstorms flash and flare for hundreds of miles along the Equator. From this God's-eye-view, I saw how fragile and infinitely precious the Earth is."

More recently, a group of Native Americans waged a valiant fight to protect land and water on the Dakota prairie they believed to be threatened by the construction of an oil pipeline. For months, they camped out on the prairie in freezing temperatures to prevent construction from progressing. Local authorities, at the instigation of the pipeline company, turned water hoses on the protesters. They arrested them for trespassing, saddling them with bonds more appropriate for criminal offenders. Still, they stood their ground.

It's hard to be as brave as those protesters. It's much easier to believe that caring for the environment is the task of high-level government officials who can negotiate a pact like the Paris Climate Accord, or set higher fuel emissions standards, and prescribe tougher testing for drinking water through the federal Environmental Protection Agency. In fact, *nothing is to be neglected* begins with us.

Somewhere along the line we became a throwaway society. It is simply cheaper and less complicated to buy a new pair of shoes than repair old ones. But is it? Sometimes I wonder what happened to all those shoes I've thrown out. Or for that matter, those eight-track tape cartridges we once owned, or the cathode ray television sets we watched before flat screen TVs came along, or those bulky desktop computers that seemed to work just fine until the iPad was invented and cell phones began to double as computers. As you read this, they lie ensconced in landfills across America. If it takes a plastic grocery bag five hundred years to decompose, it probably takes a millennium for any one of those larger items to disintegrate.

What can be done? We can do what Europeans have done for decades, and carry our groceries home in reusable bags. We can take our paper, plastics, and glass to a recycling box. We can donate our cell phones, computers, and our old appliances. Reduce, reuse, recycle is just as much a Benedictine motto these days as *Ora et Labora*. When the sisters at Mount St. Scholastica Monastery in Kansas were faced with having to tear down a sprawling brick administration building, they sold off the remnants of what they didn't need, recycled what they could use for another building they were renovating, and buried what couldn't be salvaged in their own land. Reduce, reuse, recycle.

> *The goods of the monastery, that is, its tools, clothing*
> *or anything else, should be entrusted to those whom the*
> *abbot or prioress appoints and in whose manner of life he*
> *or she has confidence . . . Whoever fails to keep the things*
> *belonging to the monastery clean or treats them carelessly*
> *should be reproved.*
>
> —FROM CHAPTER 32, "THE TOOLS AND
> GOODS OF THE MONASTERY"

In the early 1970s, Lake Erie was even more polluted than the Illinois River. Scientists described the Great Lake as being effectively dead, unable to sustain any type of fish or plant life. The sisters of Erie's Mount St. Benedict Monastery joined four other groups in suing the state of Pennsylvania to clean up the water. Today, fathers in boats with their children, along with old men and women in straw hats sitting on the shoreline, can not only catch fish in Lake Erie, they can once again eat the fish they catch.

"How is that religious?" some of Erie's residents asked Sister Joan Chittister, who was the monastery's prioress at the time. "Because we are Benedictines," she responded. "Our purpose is to present the most humane, most spiritual, most moral, most communal model of life for a world in chaos around us."

Caring for the environment is not fluff, or something to do only when it makes economic sense. In a Benedictine world, it is a sacred trust. "Imagine a miracle drug that could take away many of the stresses of modern life . . . Just take a hike in the woods or a walk in the park. No prescription necessary," Florence Williams writes in *The Nature Fix: Why Nature Makes Us Happier, Healthier and More Creative.* Studies show fifteen minutes in the woods can reduce levels of cortisol, a stress hormone, and improve cognitive performance. The scent of evergreens can act as a mild sedative. The sounds of birdsong and gurgling water can improve our mood.

More important than all this is that we are partners with nature. Together we form what the great naturalist Aldo Leopold called "a community of interdependent parts." Leopold saw firsthand what happens when the heavy hand of man reaches in to alter irrevocably the imprint of nature. He was a US Forest Service officer when the government decided gray wolves were killing too many deer and cows. Eating lunch one day on a high ridge, Leopold and a colleague spotted a wolf and some pups spring from between willows. "In those days, we never heard of passing up a chance to kill a wolf," Leopold writes in his classic book, *A Sand County Almanac.* "In a second, we were pumping lead . . . When our rifles were empty, the old wolf was down, and a pup was dragging a leg into impassable slide rocks."

The story might have ended there, but Leopold scampered down from the ridge and peered into the wolf's eyes. "We reached the old wolf in time to watch a fierce green fire dying in her eyes. I realized then, and have known ever since, that there was something new to me in those eyes—something known only to her and the mountain."

The gray wolf nearly became extinct, and along with it the animal wisdom it carried, its purpose and place in the scheme of nature. Now it is deer who have over-proliferated and eaten their way through many a mountainside "as if someone had given God new pruning shears," Leopold said. He went on to advocate a vision of the natural world based on community. A community whose members include soil, water, plants, animals—and man. He called it "the land ethic." Within this ethic, the role of *homo sapiens* changes from conqueror to plain citizen of a communal planet. This too is the Benedictine vision. *Nothing is to be neglected.*

For Reflection:

:~ How do I care for the objects entrusted to me as sacred vessels of the altar?

:~ How much do I contribute to the pollution and degradation of the environment? Are there practices I can adopt in my home and my community that would help sustain the earth, such as recycling; buying biodegradable bags and containers; using products that aren't toxic to the environment; buying locally grown produce?

:~ When I look around my neighborhood, what is the natural beauty I see? I will write a short poem, take a photograph, draw or paint a picture of what I see and what I want to preserve.

:~ How can I liberate the environment in my home of clutter, making it more of a model of Benedictine simplicity?

:~ I will read Pope Francis' encyclical *Laudate Si* to better understand how caring for the environment is also a religious act.

19

"YOUR BLESSING, PLEASE"

On Living with Awe

Wherever members meet, the junior asks the senior for a blessing . . . In this way, they do what the words of Scripture say: "They should be the first to show respect to the other." (Rom 12:10)

—FROM CHAPTER 63, "COMMUNITY RANK"

A few years ago, I had the chance to visit the Norman Rockwell Museum in Stockbridge, Massachusetts. As powerful as Rockwell's reprinted images are, to see the originals is even more moving. One of his most famous posters shows a family seated around a table. The grandparents are poised to set down a roasted turkey, just out of the oven. The image represents Rockwell's vision of "Freedom from Want," part of his famous Depression-era series for the *Saturday Evening Post* known as "The Four Freedoms."

In Rockwell's rendering, the family appears to be on the verge of reciting a blessing. The scene seems to spring out of long-ago past. With after-school soccer practices, evening meetings, and both parents working long hours, few families are able to sit down to dinner at the same time, let alone offer a blessing together. (If your family can, then you are very fortunate indeed).

The simple act of giving and receiving blessing is becoming a lost art. Monasteries are among the few places where blessings infuse daily life. They extend to visitors leaving the monastery to return home, as well as to community members about to undergo surgery or embark on a trip. Blessings are given to people about to do a job—such as serving for a week in the kitchen. In past decades, younger monks who passed an elder in a corridor were to ask for the senior's blessing. And there is of course the tradition we've already explored—the monastery porter's greeting of each visitor with either "Thanks be to God," or "Your blessing, please."

> *This porter . . . as soon as anyone knocks, or a poor person*
> *calls out, replies, "Thanks be to God" or "Your blessing,*
> *please;" then with all the gentleness that comes from the fear*
> *of God, provides a prompt answer with the warmth of love.*
> —FROM CHAPTER 66, "THE PORTER OF THE MONASTERY"

To this day, monastic communities remember members who are absent during the daily Liturgy of the Hours—offering them a blessing from afar—just as they did in the early monasteries of the 6th century. These lovely rituals are all part of the meaningful practice of blessing that weaves itself into so many ordinary occasions.

When I made my first extended visit to Mount St. Scholastica, the sisters had just finished clearing space for a new garden outside the monastery's assisted living wing so that the elderly sisters who live there could plant roses and coleus and cultivate small plots of tomatoes. The garden was only complete, though, once it had been blessed. Sister Anne Shepard, the prioress, recalled that Benedictines have always cultivated gardens. Gardens, she said, remind us of the gifts of the land. They remind us too of our need for beauty. Then she sprinkled, one by one, each flower bed, bush, and plant with holy water. Lastly, she blessed every person in attendance.

I thought of how even seemingly mundane acts like planting a garden are celebrated and mined for their deeper meaning in the Benedictine tradition. I wondered why my husband and I don't bless the little vegetable garden we plant every year by the side of our house, and the people who help with the planting. We should have blessed the new flooring we had put down in the kitchen for our tenth anniversary, and Jim, the workman, who cemented the flooring. As Wendell Berry says in his poem "How To Be a Poet," there are no unsacred places, *only sacred and desecrated places.*

On Sunday, immediately after Lauds, those beginning as well as those completing their week of service should make a profound bow in the oratory before all and ask for their prayers. Let the server completing his or her week recite this verse: "Blessed are you, Lord God, who helped me and comforted me" (Dan 3:52; Ps 86:17). After this verse has been said three times, he or she receives a blessing. Then the one beginning service follows and says: "O God, come to my assistance; O God, make haste to help me." (Ps 70:2)

—FROM CHAPTER 35, "KITCHEN SERVERS OF THE WEEK"

When we offer blessing, it is a way of expressing both awe and thanksgiving for the world we live in. I once had the opportunity to interview the late poet and theologian John O'Donohue. He wrote a wonderful book called *To Bless the Space Between Us.* O'Donohue lived in the rugged terrain around Connemara in western Ireland, where the winds blow cold, the sea roils dangerously, and the soil is hard and unforgiving. In this desolate landscape, you have to look deeply for blessing.

O'Donohue found gratitude hiding in countless corners. He wrote prayers for waking, coming home, time in solitude, and mothers-to-be. For absence, belonging, water, and wildness. For passing a graveyard, lost friends, and retirement. He included prayers for even the messes that make up the human condition: a broken relationship and the loss of trust—for wrapped in those disappointments might be a hidden gift. This is how we bless the space between us. We don't need to be in a house of worship, nor do we need to wear a cleric's collar.

When my mother was still alive and I was traveling frequently for my work at the *Wall Street Journal* and later PBS-TV, she would call the night before my trip and say, "Good trip, safe trip, God bless." I can't tell you how many times her little blessing fortified my spirits on bumpy airplane landings, in overcrowded train stations, and through snowy driving conditions.

Now that she's gone, my husband and I give each other the blessing whenever either of us heads out of town. My friends who know about the tradition ask for the blessing when they are traveling. It's not that the words contain magic. They don't. What they do is free us to expect good.

Members sent on a journey will ask the prioress or abbot
and the community to pray for them. All absent members

*should always be remembered at the closing prayer of the
Work of God.*

—FROM CHAPTER 67, "MEMBERS SENT ON A JOURNEY"

One of the most moving moments of my wedding ceremony came when the priest officiating sprinkled holy water and said a prayer over both our rings. That blessing drove home to me that my wedding ring isn't merely a beautiful piece of jewelry, it's also a symbol of the sacred space that was about to enfold the two of us for the rest of our lives.

At Mount St. Scholastica (and at many women's Benedictine monasteries), there is a tradition in which every visitor who makes a presentation or completes work for the community is sent home with a sung blessing. The community members all stand, raise both arms, and sing:

*May the Lord look upon you with kindness.
May the Lord fill your heart with holy peace.
God's love be forever within you.
May the Lord always bless you and keep you.*

As a young journalist, I was advised early on in my career by a senior female editor, "Whatever you do, *never* let them see you cry." Whenever I've been fortunate enough to receive the Mount sisters' blessing, my former editor's advice flies out the window. The tears come freely, and publicly. Blessing does that. The earliest monastics saw blessings as ever-renewing signs of grace in our often-confounding lives.

Like those elder monks in ancient times, may we never fail to bless those who cross our paths. And like the monastic porter, may we never fear to ask, "Your blessing, please."

For Reflection:

- ∾ What were the occasions in which I received a blessing, perhaps an anointing before surgery, or during a retreat? What did it feel like to be blessed?

- ∾ Have I ever given someone a blessing? What was the experience like?

- ∾ Taking a cue from John O'Donohue, I will write blessings for three things I consider gifts in my life right now. For example, O'Donohue wrote blessings for work, for meeting a stranger, for a birthday, for mothers, fathers, brothers, and sisters.

- ∾ I will write blessings for three things that challenge me. O'Donohue wrote a blessing for failure, for loneliness, for the family and friends of a person who committed suicide.

- ∾ Is Wendell Berry right that there are no unsacred places, only sacred and desecrated places? What places are sacred to me? What desecrated places can I name? (One might think of parts of Syria, Iraq, Israel or other countries where violence is a daily occurrence). Can I find something to bless in those places?

20

A SCHOOL FOR
THE LORD'S SERVICE

On Finding Meaning in Our Work

Therefore we intend to establish a school for the Lord's service. In drawing up its regulations, we hope to set down nothing harsh, nothing burdensome."

—FROM THE PROLOGUE

A key struggle of my career has centered on how to strike a balance between doing the work I love and living a more mindful, contemplative life. There is an ancient wisdom story from the sayings of the desert fathers and mothers that showed me a path forward. It crystalizes in just a few sentences my desire to build a monastery of the heart that can also be my refuge in the work world.

A merchant once came to a monastic elder for advice about his business.

"As the fish perishes on dry land, so you too perish when you get entangled in the world," the monk said. "The fish must return to the water, and you must return to the spirit."

The merchant was deeply troubled by these words.

"Are you saying I must give up my business and live in a monastery?" he asked.

"Definitely not," the elder said. "I am telling you to hold on to your business and go into your heart."

The novelist Joshua Ferris once described the workplace as "life's strangest environment, the one we pretend is normal five days a week." And yet, it is the place where many of us spend the bulk of our waking hours. St. Benedict called the monastery—his workplace—*a school for the Lord's service.* For many of us, the office, the store, the factory, the courtroom, and the newsroom aren't merely places where we put in time. We seek more from them than a paycheck. We seek meaning. We want to work from the heart.

My earliest vision of work derives from the jobs my parents held. My father, a truck driver, woke at 3 A.M. each day to load ten-gallon barrels of roofing cement he delivered to businesses in New York, New Jersey, and Pennsylvania. My mother stood ankle-deep in red rubber boots in a pool of gray water, hosing down cucumbers at Wachsburg's Pickle Works. Their work was labor. I decided early on that this would not be my work.

The use of all one's talents in the pursuit of excellence. That is how the Greeks defined happiness. I decided that is what work would be for me. I soon got the break of a lifetime, or so it seemed. the *Washington Post*, one of the largest newspapers in the country, wanted to hire me as a reporter as soon as I graduated from college. None other than Bob Woodward of Watergate fame would be one of my editors.

My parents drove me to DC in our family's beat-up Chevy Caprice. They returned home to New Jersey the night before I was to start my job. That evening, I sat alone in a restaurant eating an egg salad sandwich. I began to cry right there at the table. Never had I felt so isolated, so in over my head. I quickly found an antidote for my feelings of loneliness and anxiety. I threw myself into work. I stayed late at the office most weeknights, and lived for those days I could see my byline on the front page of the paper. I thought I was following the definition of happiness. *The use of all one's talents in the pursuit of excellence.* Only the happiness wasn't there. I had a job that included my life, not a life that included my job.

I was so clueless that I thought happiness would lie in landing a job at an even bigger newspaper. After seven years of my self-imposed grind at the *Washington Post*, I was hired by the *Wall Street Journal*, then the largest-circulation newspaper in the country. I spent my first years at the *Journal* in the Chicago bureau. I loved the great spirit of that city and enjoyed my beat, covering the airline industry and writing human interest stories for the paper's front page. Soon though, my familiar pattern reemerged of placing work above everything else, including my spiritual, emotional, and physical well-being. There were just enough fringe benefits to keep the spiral going: I won numerous awards for my reporting, though a kind of inner deadness would always set in again.

Ora et labora—pray and work—is the Benedictine motto. The phrase doesn't specifically appear in *The Rule,* but its prescription for balance suffuses every chapter. Monastics need to work, as much as they need to pray, Benedict says. If they don't survive by the work of their hands, they shouldn't be called monks. But he also insists there should be specified periods for *both* prayer and labor. This isn't something to leave to chance or tack on hastily at the end of a hectic work week. Contemplation and action are two sides of the same scale. We aren't to shirk our duties, leaving our messes for someone else, or whittle away the hours daydreaming. But neither are we to work ourselves to distraction, or into an early grave.

> *When they live by the labor of their hands, as our ancestors and the apostles did, they are really monastics. Yet, all things are to be done with moderation."*
>
> —FROM CHAPTER 48, "THE DAILY MANUAL LABOR"

Plato and Aristotle both believed daily work interfered with the pursuits of the mind. The Romans of Benedict's era denigrated most forms of work, leaving it to the slave classes. Indeed, slaves at one time in Roman history outnumbered free men. *The Rule,* by contrast, elevates work to a level of holiness. St. Benedict refers to community prayer as the *Opus Dei,* "the work of God." In that way, he sets prayer—seeking God, cultivating an interior life—as the central work of the monastery. This is not to confuse work with prayer. In keeping with *The Rule,* our work life flows from our life of prayer. One supports the other.

In many ways, I was fortunate in that I always knew I wanted to be a writer. I chose journalism (a profession these days too often wrongly maligned) because I saw it as way to use whatever writing talent I have in the service of others. I've always looked upon my work as more of a calling than a means to earn a living. Journalists are keepers of a sacred trust. We serve as witnesses to crucial moments in history. Like clergy and medical professionals, we often accompany people at critical moments in their lives. We are able to give voice to the needs of people whose voices society so often muffles—the poor, the marginalized, the disenfranchised. As one of my editors at the *Wall Street Journal* used to say, the role of the journalist is to "comfort the afflicted and afflict the comfortable." My mistake at various times was taking that commission to the extreme. I let my work take over my life to the exclusion of silence, solitude, and the reflective times necessary to nourish the soul.

The Rule offers instructions for working in ways that don't starve the soul, but feed it. *Be the first to show respect to the other*, St. Benedict says. *Listen.* To the artisans of the monastery (and by extension, those of us in business today) he says charge for goods and services *what is just*. Consider that last one in connection with pharmaceutical companies that demand monopolistic prices of as much as $1,000 per pill on life-saving drugs.

> *The evil of avarice must have no part in establishing prices.*
> —FROM CHAPTER 57, "THE ARTISANS OF THE MONASTERY"

St. Benedict tells those in management positions to *lead more by example than words*. Avoid favoritism. Allow newcomers to the organization a say, along with the top brass. *Let those who are not strong have help, so that they may serve without distress.* Give to *each according to his need.* Just as he decreed community members should get a daily minimum of seven hours of sleep, to all of us who work, he says remember to take enough rest. Care for the resources and tools given to you *as if they are the sacred vessels of the altar*. Avoid speaking ill of others. Above all, he says, *Your way of acting should be different from the world's way; the love of Christ must come before all else.*

In an age in which 86 percent of American workers say they are dissatisfied with their jobs, and 82 percent acknowledge they lack an adequate work-life balance, these prescriptions in *The Rule* aren't mere platitudes. They are tools for transforming the way we work.

Mary Oliver has a wonderful poem called "Messenger" that begins, "My work is loving the world." It is a sentiment that flows directly from *The Rule*. If our work isn't about loving, then perhaps it isn't worth doing. This doesn't limit us to certain professions— say work in the clergy, medicine, social work, and other helping professions, or even my own beloved profession, journalism. We can all love the world through our work.

I remember moderating a panel of women executives a few years ago. One of the panelists was a vice president of a major airline. She described the intense scrutiny she endured as a female in senior management. She said that often the highlight of her day is to head for the Chick-Fil-A down the road, where the gregarious cashier always has a kind, positive word for customers. She completes each transaction by wishing them a "blessed day." That cashier is "loving the world" through her work. Angie and Josie at the clothing store where I worked in high school, who transformed the dingy stock room into a safe, nurturing environment, made their work "loving the world."

*What is not possible to us by nature, let us ask the Holy
One to supply by the help of grace . . . Then, while there
is still time, while we are in this body and have time to
accomplish all these things by the light of life, we must
run and do now what will profit us forever.*

—FROM THE PROLOGUE

New York Times columnist David Brooks wrote a wonderful
book called *The Road to Character* in which he explores true success. He draws a distinction between "resume virtues" and "eulogy
virtues." Resume virtues describe the skills we bring to the mar-
ketplace. Eulogy virtues are what define our character. They are
the virtues people talk about when we die. Were we kind, brave,
honest, faithful? Were we capable of great love?

"People on the road to inner light do not find their vocations by
asking, what do I want from life?" Brooks writes. "They ask, how
can I match my intrinsic talents with one of the world's deep needs?"

How can I match my talents with the world's deepest needs? I started
this reflection on the spirituality of work with the classic Greek
definition of happiness. *The use of all one's talents in the pursuit of
excellence.* There is another Greek word that better defines what the
aim of our work should be. It is *eudaimonia. Eudaimonia* describes
a sense of meaning and well-being. It comes when the work I do
profits not only me, but others as well. When we make *eudaimonia*
our aim, we move closer to achieving not only the Greeks' definition of happiness, but the measure of true success.

Our work is loving the world.

For Reflection:

:~ When was the last time I felt *eudaimonia*, a sense of meaning and well-being, about the work I do? How can I cultivate that sense day to day?

:~ What does it mean to me personally to make my work "loving the world?"

:~ How would I rate my work-life balance? What can I start doing today to bring that ratio into better balance?

:~ St. Benedict called "idleness" the enemy of the soul. How would I describe the difference between idleness and leisure, rest, or relaxation?

:~ What are some of the ways I blend being an active, work-oriented Martha/Martin with the Mary/Matthew of my inner self who dwells in quiet, meditation, and silence?

21

"I'VE NEVER BEEN WHERE I AM NOT"

On Contemplation

Let them prefer nothing whatever to Christ.
—FROM CHAPTER 72, "THE GOOD ZEAL OF MONASTICS"

People often ask me, what is contemplation? It is one of those words—like charisma and creativity—that defies easy definition. We know it when we experience it. People often refer to monastics as living "the contemplative life," as if somehow a life of mindfulness and reflection is off limits to the rest of us. Contemplation isn't the topic of a chapter in *The Rule,* in the way that humility, silence, and prayer are. But its presence seeps into every chapter, because to live by the *The Rule* is to live an awakened life. That is as apt a definition as any of contemplation.

The great 20th-century poet William Carlos Williams was a pediatrician who scribbled his poems on prescription pads in between house calls and his patients' office visits. "I take my poems where I find them," he once said. As a doctor operating a medical practice, he upended a popular notion that poets are people disengaged from the pursuits of ordinary life. I like to say I take my moments of contemplation where I find them. It might be in the middle of Chicago's busy Michigan Avenue shopping district, at O'Hare Airport waiting to catch a plane, or sitting at my writing desk.

We—or at least I—have a tendency to make hard things simple and simple things hard. Thomas Merton said the contemplative life boils down to three tiny words: *now, here,* and *this*. If we live aware of the present moment, wherever we are, fully engaged in the *this* we are doing, then we are living a contemplative life. We will have nothing to regret. *Now. Here. This.*

Merton offered a definition of contemplation that is simple, yet challenging. He said it is a way of being "fully active, fully aware, fully alive." I like that he included *active* as well, because I have found being contemplative doesn't mean we don't or can't live dynamic and energetic lives. It means that we bring a reflective, attentive attitude to whatever we do.

We need both contemplation *and* action. (Remember *ora et labora*—work *and* prayer). One informs the other. Contemplation without action would be like driving a car without wheels. And action without contemplation would be like building a house without a blueprint. Contemplation alone, Merton warned, doesn't feed the hungry, teach the uneducated, clothe the poor, or stop the violence. We need the prayers of monasteries, yes. But we need actors to carry out those prayers too. "We must work together," Merton wrote, "I with my books and prayers, you with your work and prayers. Separately we are incomplete, together we are strong with the strength of God."

Edward Hirsch is one of my favorite poets—and not only because he grew up outside my beloved adopted home of Chicago. He is someone who combines a day job as head of the Guggenheim Foundation in New York with the reflective attentiveness needed to write poetry. In his poem, "I Am Going to Start Living Like a Mystic," he debunks the notion that it takes an other-worldly persona or environment to live contemplatively. He starts out in the poem by pulling on a green wool sweater and walking across a park during a snowfall. It is dusk. He counts the trees—twenty-seven of them—and imagines each one is a stop on a pilgrimage.

He examines the few remaining leaves, as if they were pages of a sacred text. He kneels to observe a "vanquished" squirrel, and stares into the surface of a pond to see forms taking shape there. He scours the sky, looking for signs of the constellations. Finally, he begins the long trek back to where he started.

> *I will walk home alone with the deep alone*
> *A disciple of shadows in praise of the mysteries*

In this loving act of careful observation, he encounters the mystery at the center of all things. He becomes an everyday mystic. It started with simply pulling on a wool sweater and taking a walk. Much simpler than anyone could have expected. His attentiveness brings him to a place of praise and thanksgiving. It reminds me of something my friend Brother Paul Quenon of the Abbey of Gethsemani once said. "Contemplation is just a big fat word for gratitude."

> *Just as there is a wicked zeal of bitterness which separates*
> *from God . . . so there is a good zeal which separates*
> *from evil and leads to God and everlasting life.*

—FROM CHAPTER 72, "THE GOOD ZEAL OF MONASTICS"

I look upon contemplation now, not as something to be worked at or aspired to, but as an attitude I carry within me wherever I am. A case of what the late Benedictine writer Imogene Baker once described as "Be where you are and do what you're doing."

In her book *Long Quiet Highway: Waking Up in America*, Natalie Goldberg writes of watching her beloved Zen teacher wait at a curbside for his ride to arrive. When he's told his driver is running late, he doesn't appear worried or impatient. He simply nods and says, "Thank you."

"What was he doing while he was standing there?" Goldberg's friend wants to know.

"Nothing, he was standing. Until I saw that kind of equanimity, I didn't think it was possible," Goldberg says.

Just standing. Doing nothing. Letting the moment soak in, which looks a lot like contemplation.

Toward the end of his life, my friend, the Benedictine Abbot Owen Purcell, told me he regretted having wasted so much time rehashing the past and worrying about the future. He wrote a little limerick to help keep his attention centered on the present moment. The *now, here, this.*

> *I've never been where I am not*
> *I've always been where I am*
> *Goodbye to the past that was*
> *Hello to the now I'm in*

Now that's living like a mystic.

For Reflection:

:~ Thomas Merton offers a definition of contemplation, as does Imogene Baker. How would I define contemplation?

:~ How do I take my contemplative moments where I find them (at work, at home, on my daily commute)?

:~ Having decided to "live like a mystic," I will take a short walk. How is the experience different from a normal stroll?

:~ I will write a short limerick like Abbot Owen Purcell's, or a three-line haiku poem that can serve as a reminder to live more contemplatively.

:~ Contemplation has been compared to waking up. What do I need to wake up to in my daily life?

22

ALWAYS BEGINNING

On Conversatio Morum

Then, with Christ's help, keep this little rule that we have written for beginners. After that, you can set out for the loftier summits . . . and under God's protection, you will reach them.

—FROM CHAPTER 73, "THIS RULE ONLY
A BEGINNING OF PERFECTION"

The Rule of St. Benedict isn't merely a text. If we take it to heart, it is a journey into the self. Like any journey, it begins with a single step—in this case, the word *Listen*. Most texts close with "The End." *The Rule* finishes by proclaiming its end is a beginning. As we travel into our interior, we are on are on a journey with no foreseeable ending. We are always beginning because we are voyagers on a road to *conversatio*.

Conversatio morum are two words that aren't spelled out explicitly in *The Rule,* but infuse every line, every chapter. They are the key to living a Benedictine life. In chapter 58, "The Procedure for Receiving Members," there is an oblique reference to *conversatio.* It comes as St. Benedict describes the three vows each member of the monastic community takes: stability (to remain in the same community for life); obedience (to one's superiors and in service toward one another in the community); and *fidelity to the monastic way of life.* That last one is the closest *The Rule* comes to spelling out *conversatio morum.*

To anyone who tries to live a Benedictine life, these words are as familiar as morning. But to me, when I began making my visits to Mount St. Scholastica and studying *The Rule,* they were both exotic and new. Like hundreds of pilgrims before me, I came to this monastery in America's heartland seeking personal transformation. I could sense by the reverence with which these two words were spoken that they contained at least a piece of what I was searching for. I guessed the words meant something akin to "conversion of morals," and soon learned that the more common translation is "conversion of life." One of the Mount sisters suggested I might begin my Benedictine journey by exploring what *conversatio* could mean for me. I headed for the Google search engine. There I found several nicely-boxed definitions:

A daily reshaping of the mind and heart.

Being broken and renewed, being overwhelmed and raised up: a willingness to suffer, to be confused on the way to new life.

Being in the hands of the living God, the God who always surprises us, always shatters our expectations, the God who surpasses imagination.

From versatio con, *as in turning with.*

I was particularly drawn to that last definition. I appreciate the notion of turning because turning connotes change, and when it comes to the spiritual life, there is so much I'd like to change about myself. I'd like to be more patient, less temperamental, more accepting, less judgmental. I would like to be someone capable of seeing beyond the obvious.

I once received an important lesson about *conversatio* from my friend Sister Thomasita Homan of Mount St. Scholastica. I told her that I liked myself better when I was visiting the monastery. There, I was calm, patient, I didn't lose my temper. It was often a different story when I returned home to my "regular" life. One day, shortly after returning from a two-week visit to the Mount, I argued with my beautiful husband. It was a stupid, totally unnecessary argument. In frustration, I called Sister Thomasita and asked "Why is it when I'm at the monastery, I'm a different person, and when I'm home, I can't seem to be that way with the person I love most in the world? Why do I have so much trouble living *conversatio* in my daily life?" She told me something I've never forgotten.

"You are living *conversatio*," she said. "Your struggle, that's the *conversatio.*"

Sister Thomasita called *conversatio* a "continuous conversation with life." That gave me hope. I don't have to be perfect. I just have to be human.

It is interesting that the desert fathers and mothers often referred to themselves as beginners. The most revered monks were often the most reluctant to claim the title of "teacher," "elder," or "master." They understood that *conversatio* isn't a sudden tectonic shift. *Conversatio* is more like the way water eventually etches away at a shoreline. It is slow, steady, daily work that often results in infinitesimal change, but change nonetheless.

I've come to view *conversatio* not as the work of one year, or five, or even a season of life. It is the work of a lifetime—one that operates on the same principle as those traditional Russian dolls within dolls. As soon as *conversatio* opens one door in the heart, it is time to walk through another, and another.

As Bob Dylan's grandmother told him, "everyone you'll ever meet is fighting a hard battle." That hard battle is the grinder of each person's own *conversatio*. When I feel myself getting frustrated with people who aren't acting as I think they should; when I have to interview someone whose personality grates on me (and mine probably grates on them as well!); when I feel a coworker or supervisor is placing an unreasonable demand on me, it helps to remember that all of them are fighting their own hard battles. I can see my own struggles in them. They are living out their *conversatio*, just like me and everyone else.

My friend Father Larry Janowski is a poet and Franciscan priest. He beautifully captures the spirit of *conversatio* in a poem he wrote called "Communion Procession." As people step up to the altar to take communion from his hand, he reflects on their individual lives and sees each as a member in the collective "body of Christ."

> *The body of Christ . . .*
> *. . . must have been working in the garden*
> *. . . smells of playground sweat*
> *. . . is missing two fingers*
> *. . . must be six months pregnant*
> *. . . cannot look me in the eye*
> *. . . is still grieving his wife*
> *. . . has made three months of sobriety*
> *. . . has a baby in each arm*
> *. . . is growing her hair back*
> *. . . has a smile like fireworks*

> . . . *must be two inches taller than last week*
> . . . *has a son in Afghanistan*
> . . . *needs confidence to come out of the closet*
> . . . *should have divorced him years ago*
> . . . *has hands nearly translucent*
> . . . *has been giggling all through Mass*
> . . . *tries hard to hide the Parkinson's*
> . . . *reminds me of my grandfather*
> . . . *has skin the color of coffee*
> . . . *still hasn't the knack of her wheelchair*
> . . . *has to let go of that anger*
> . . . *can't remember to turn off his cell phone*
> . . . *has more faith than I*
> . . . *surely mustn't realize what that T shirt says*
> . . . *is beautiful*
>
> *Amen*

All of them fighting their hard battles. All of them living out their own *conversatio*.

St. Benedict never promises living *The Rule* will be easy. He doesn't say we can accomplish what he calls *the cultivation of virtues* all at once, or all on our own. In fact, he's pretty clear that this can be accomplished only in the company of others with whom we link arms and draw support. It also takes massive amounts of grace—those mysterious blessings that arrive as pure, inexplicable gift.

The prologue to *The Rule* ends with a beautiful passage that extends both a hope and a promise:

> *Do not be daunted immediately by fear and run away*
> *from the road that leads to salvation. It is bound to be*

> *narrow at the outset. But as we progress in this way of*
> *life and faith, we shall run on the path of God's com-*
> *mandments, our hearts overflowing with the inexpress-*
> *ible delight of love.*

—FROM THE PROLOGUE

Our hearts overflowing with the inexpressible delight of love. Who wouldn't be grateful for even a modicum of that kind of delight every day? But few things worth doing are ever easy. It is why we are always beginners. A young monk approached an elder and said, "Try as I might to be good-tempered, chaste and sober, I keep on sinning." The older monk replied, "Brother, the spiritual life is this: I rise up and I fall down. I rise up and I fall down." The young monk stayed and persevered. Hopefully, so will we.

For Reflection:

:~ What is it I must *turn* in my own life in order to progress on the way of *conversatio?*

:~ If I am experiencing stress in a relationship with someone, can I envision the hard battles that person may be facing? How might those battles be part of his or her *conversatio?*

:~ Looking at how others have defined *conversatio morum,* how might I define it for myself?

:~ The road to *conversatio* is bound to be narrow at times, St. Benedict says. How do I react when I am feeling daunted?

:~ St. Benedict suggests if we stay on the path of *conversatio,* our hearts will eventually "overflow with the inexpressible delight of love." When have I experienced that depth of love? Did it grow out of a disappointment that turned into an unexpected blessing? Did it tiptoe into my life, a quiet thing? Did it come as a gradual realization that my entire life has been the uncovering of a continuous series of sometimes hidden blessings?

AFTERWORD

Many, many thousands of book titles begin with "How to...." Critics, snipers, humorists, reviewers, and the professionally bored find it easy to dismiss everything in this category. Certainly the author and publisher of *How to Live* had to know the risks they were taking by adding one more title to the list. It was even more daring to link "How to" with the word "Live," which represents the most challenging concept this side of "Die." We picture that authors who hope to be of service to readers would compete for attention with emphatic, boisterous, noisy claims. Yet readers of *How to Live* will treasure this approach precisely because it is marked by quiet and simplicity.

Anyone who doubts that claim might reread this book and seek to find passages that would suggest author Valente offers quick cures for those who are not sure "how to live" and are therefore troubled and frustrated. They will find the opposite: recall the places to which she would guide the seeker. For starters, or enders, think of her imaginative literary trips to Mount St. Scholastica in Kansas. As a son of the Plains, I have nothing against and very much for places like Kansas. But the promise of such underpopulated locales has to be revealed through attention to the promises God tucks away *anywhere*. Revelation appears here not only in monastery chapels but also in the quiet transactions between a husband and wife and with stepchildren. "Revelation" thus can refer to what God would promise and does achieve for those who are attentive.

The author's use of *The Rule of St. Benedict* is key to the unfolding here, because for centuries believers have been cheered and startled by its wise offerings, many of them so apparently ordinary that the hasty may overlook them on a first reading. (I intrude with a plea: do what those who follow *The Rule* do: they revisit it and let themselves get reached again and again by its phrases and counsels.)

For one sample, notice St. Benedict and those inspired by him, now immediately and notably, the contemporary writer Valente, being caught up short by a Benedictine phrase as simple as "day by day." Here we learn to think that one of the days being noticed will be the day of one's death. Fear not! reads, or hears, the increasingly patient reader. *Reader?* I was ready to write about the increasingly patient *listener*. But the *Rule* and its commentator are clear of their purpose when they counsel taking the path of the reader to someone who here confesses (p. 48): "I talk and talk and talk," until she shocks herself when she notices that she is advocating for silence!

Self-confessed workaholic and overachiever Valente quite confidently shows that she regards her readers as having her typical kind of problems. The life stories that lurk in her paragraphs remain to be of help to all who read and thus hear *The Rule* and this particular contemporary counsel from the prologue (p. 12): "Listen carefully my daughter, my son to my instructions and attend to them with the ear of your heart." We have yet more to hear as we *listen* to the pages.

MARTIN E. MARTY, emeritus, The University of Chicago